101 Reasons to Own the World's Greatest Investment

Warren Buffett's
Berkshire Hathaway

101 Reasons to Own the World's Greatest Investment

Warren Buffett's
Berkshire Hathaway

Robert P. Miles

John Wiley & Sons, Inc.
New York • Chichester • Weinheim • Brisbane • Singapore • Toronto

Published by John Wiley & Sons, Inc.
Published simultaneously in Canada.

This publication is designed to provide accurate and authoritative information in regard to the subject matter covered. It is sold with the understanding that the publisher is not engaged in rendering professional services. If professional advice or other expert assistance is required, the services of a competent professional person should be sought.

Library of Congress Cataloging-in-Publication Data

Miles, Robert P.
    101 reasons to own the world's greatest investment: Warren Buffett's Berkshire Hathaway / Robert P. Miles.
       p. cm.
    Rev. ed. of: The world's greatest investment. c1999.
    "Recommended web sites": p.
    Includes bibliographical references and index.
    ISBN 0-471-41123-X (cloth : acid-free paper)
    1. Berkshire Hathaway Inc. 2. Buffett, Warren. 3. Investments—United States. 4. Mutual funds—United States. I. Title: One hundred one reasons to own the world's greatest investment. II. Title: One hundred and one reasons to own the world's greatest investment. III. Title.

HG4930.M55 2001
332.63'27—dc21

00-065285

*To My Daughter
Marybeth*

A Message to Children, Especially My Daughter

As a parent who loves you with all of my heart, I have attempted to pass on what I have learned about the world of investing. Every time I bring up the subject your eyes glaze over and you couldn't be more bored. It pains you to listen and I don't want to turn you off or away from a very important subject about which is difficult to make fun. You give me fifteen minutes each year to talk about your annual stock selection, what the Dow is and why it is important, investment terms, investment beliefs, short term vs long term. May I take two of my fifteen minutes here?

I want to teach you what took me 30 years to understand. I feel it is my responsibility to help you understand something that is simple but not easy. I want to protect you from the financial educators that have more of their self-interest at heart more than yours. I want you to instinctively know what is the financial truth. To recognize it. To understand it. To be able to explain it to your sixth-grade classmates.

You tell me that your friend Kendall has a school backpack sign that says, 'Shopping: the art of buying something that you don't need, with money you don't have, to impress people you don't care about.'

Let me try to explain investing in the same terms, 'Investing: the science and fine art of buying companies that everyone needs, with money that you have saved, for the benefit of people you care very much about.'

I don't think that investing needs to be complex or boring. If you can't understand the simple concepts at a sixth-grade level then you shouldn't invest no matter what your age.

An important part of maturing is denying yourself something today so you have more tomorrow. To deny yourself pleasure today so that your family has a better future. To realize that you can't be good at everything and some things like investing may be best in the care of others, either in passive form like an index fund or active form like an individual stock.

You will be way ahead of the game if you learn to buy a few widely respected companies and to death do you part. A concept difficult for most adults, let alone children.

I realize the best education is by example. The difficulty with investing and taxes is they are generally very private affairs, not the subject of day to day living and not terribly exciting to a preteen, teenager, and young adult.

I doubt that this collection makes investing any more exciting for you but hopefully attempts in a very small way to educate, inform, amuse, and intrigue.

Acknowledgments

First and foremost I need to thank my friend, attorney, and CPA, John Baum of Farmington Hills, Michigan for making this book happen. His daily phone calls were invaluable to the creation of this series. Some of the reasons are his alone and some are partly his. This collection is mostly a collaborative project with his input and my writing. John's wife, Paulette is concerned that he is a Berkshire stalker, maybe a little excessive compulsive, but mostly just passionate about this wonderful company.

A big thank you to Amelia Campbell for her daily guidance, support, and encouragement, and for her discounted hourly rate for advice, comfort, questioning, and editing.

To the Motley Fool *(www.fool.com)* for providing a vehicle for this series to be created, debated, and explored, and for honoring my work with a place below the frequently asked questions about Berkshire Hathaway.

For three and a half months I posted "101 Reasons To Own Berkshire Hathaway" one at a time on the Internet and feel as though many individuals helped with this collection. I don't know them to thank them by name but list their pseudonyms here as a small way of showing my appreciation. The Sandman, (my first and most loyal supporter), DerekG, (who thought I might be Mr. Buffett himself), Palafo, HainesR, InfernalElk, jgvoeling, Langame, FoolLynn, Starling, Phoolish1, Weaselboy2, StockpickerSteve, douffas, ftex, lgnterm, sometomfoolery, Bkeaton, ahlegren, damguy, jitterbug81, dr_e, hunzi(who took the time to index my project), JeanDavid, geodelaney (for organizing the Omaha dinner), DCUnited, Zamboni, Tastychap, Slick63, CTM, DanShep, bballen, jtholmes, edmulroy, terence2, bk777, stayput, Dale0221, aloper, baumie, lrush, FourStarDave,

raintreecounty, jslar98, TMFtwitty, ziziwin, max2001, Russel-Maynard, StanDev, Seasonless, ruleslayer, endo, ziggy29, hielmerus, valueofwhat, mkarim, travist, douglas403, twent, Tfoolery, Rickson9 (JimC www.ticonline.com), bi3ll, wmanos, trickb, dillbuch, tedwarin, FOOLROF, jmls, Medavis850, lungfish, rvbrablish, lpacer, rscharmm, fledginginvestor, SED222, TMFSelena, gmulaw, showme, DennisMcC, Chrisbafool, bobrosen, TMFcheese, Paul/sea/tyo, genemont, azathoth, mgregg, and yma2z.

I know some of you enjoyed my work and helped me along, others wished I spent my time doing something else. Some thought I dominated the message board and some thought I should have been more interactive. My apologies to those that didn't feel that I fit into their agenda. I return your board back to you for safekeeping until the next "fool" takes up the challenge of writing a series on the Internet.

To all the fine people who make up Berkshire's first Internet club on AOL, the Yellow Brkers.

Thank you to Andy Kilpatrick, author of *Of Permanent Value: the Story of Warren Buffett*. He encouraged me to publish my work. And to Alice Schroeder, the first security analyst with guts to begin covering Berkshire Hathaway. She kindly read my work and pointed out where some of my numbers were wrong.

To Debbie Bosanek for helping me at the Berkshire corporate office and confirming facts and figures.

To Kurt Loft, of the Tampa Tribune, for agreeing to edit this series after it was completed on the Internet without knowing much about Mr. Buffett or Berkshire. He tells me that my spelling errors and grammar mistakes lit up like a Christmas Tree.

To Carmella DeBiasi for her original edition book cover design and typesetting. And, to Lee Bakunin, Ken Roberts, and Beth Murphy for their kindness in pointing out misspellings and simple grammar errors. To Ricc Rollins for being my book doctor. To Will Harrell for his "lunchtime" advice. To John Zemanovich for my first opportunity to speak along with the other Buffett authors.

To Janet Wright for her support and encouragement. To Janet Lowe, author of an assortment of financial and business-related books, for being my role model and mentor. Without her, John Wiley and Sons Publishers would not have published this hardcover edition.

To all the folks at Wiley, particularly Tim Hand for recommending my self-published effort. To Deb Englander, a gifted editor, talented motivator, and lightning-fast decision maker. To Joan O'Neil, publisher, for believing in my work. To Meredith McGinnis, marketing manager with a quick grasp on how to capture book buyers. To Alexia Meyers for her top-notch production of this work.

To Andrea Pedolsky from Altair Literary Agency for guiding me through my first book contract.

To all of the ever-expanding Berkshire operating managers, particularly Lou Simpson, Al Ueltschi, Tony Nicely, Ralph Schey, Stan Lipsey, Ajit Jain, Eliot and Barry Tatelman, Frank Rooney, Susan Jacques, Irv Blumkin, Bill Child, Harrold Melton, Randy Watson, Melvyn Wolff, Jeff Comment, Chuck Huggins, and Rich Santulli.

To Berkshire board member Malcolm "Kim" Chace, and Don Graham of the Washington Post, for their interesting insights.

To my Mother for giving me a love of books. To my beloved step-father, Leo for being my investment sounding board, a ready ear, and a loving parent. May you rest in peace.

To Charlie Munger for helping create Berkshire and for his wonderful speeches and annual meeting comments.

And most of all, my thanks to Mr. Warren Buffett for granting permission to reprint his copyrighted material and as the mastermind behind such a wonderful company.

Contents

Contents

Contents

Contents

Contents

Foreword

We are constantly amazed at the things that develop from interaction and participation in online discussion boards. That's largely how The Motley Fool was born, and it's how this book was born, too. Our entire Motley Fool enterprise essentially sprang from a group of investors, passionate about the subject of money, sharing their thoughts online back in 1994. Four years later, among the thousands of discussions happening at Fool.com was one dedicated to Warren Buffett's company, Berkshire Hathaway. And one day, on the Berkshire Hathaway discussion board, a poster named "SimpleInvestor" showed up, and began a string of posts entitled "101 Reasons to Own Berkshire Hathaway." The rest is history.

"SimpleInvestor" was (and is!) Bob Miles, of course, and while some may have expected him to run out of energy or ideas after perhaps reason number 37 ("Lowers Shareholders Expectations"), he didn't. He made it to reason number 101 (and beyond) and his series proved so popular and well received that it soon became a book–this book.

One of our founding beliefs at The Motley Fool is a belief in the power of learning together. Bob Miles and his 101 Reasons exemplify this spirit. He has taught thousands of people in our community by sharing his thoughts on Berkshire Hathaway the company, BRK.A and BRK.B the investments, and Warren Buffett the investor. The Fool community has surely taught Bob, too, as they reacted to and discussed each of his 101 concepts as they came. The resulting book is not only a great learning tool for investors, it's a great example of the benefits of the Internet and the future of how information is exchanged. Who could have forecast that Bob or anyone could write a wonderful book incrementally, online, with contributions from outside readers well before the book was published? A new creative process—a wonderful one—is being loosed upon the world!

Now, for those who think that there's a limit to how much a single company and investor—no matter how great—can be discussed, Bob's book proves otherwise. The same holds true for our Berkshire discussion group at The Fool; at the time of this writing, that group has generated more than 40,000 posts from thousands of people interested in Mr. Buffett and his company. That's the equivalent of more than 50 full-length books on the subject. The beauty of Bob's work is that he infused that discussion group with creative energy and ideas, and benefited from the additional perspectives of his audience.

The result is a book covering a range of topics, including thoughts on deferred taxes, rich balance sheets, book value growth, value investing, capital allocation and international exposure. It also includes other colorful topics: loyal shareholders, the chairman's mortality, plain annual reports, lazy investor approaches, truth in advertising, independent thought, uncommon-common-sense business thinking, and a long series of life lessons. You'll certainly learn a lot about Warren Buffett and his remarkable company in this book. But the truth is you'll also gain a lot of insights into other companies. Because so many of Warren Buffett's experiences and teachings are relevant throughout the commercial world, many of the issues that Bob examines can be applied to other businesses—public and private.

Warren Buffett's long-term track record with Berkshire Hathaway is nothing short of amazing. The more any of us can learn about Buffett and his approach to investing, the more successful we're likely to be in our own investing. Bob Miles' effort here is a fine resource for the student of Berkshire Hathaway and the student of business. We're thrilled that its seed was planted at The Motley Fool. It is our hope that this book will inspire you to learn about great companies (join the discussion at www.Fool.com) and become engaged in your own financial future.

David and Tom Gardner
Co-Founders of The Motley Fool, Fool.com

101 Reasons to Own the World's Greatest Investment

Warren Buffett's
Berkshire Hathaway

March 29, 1999

Mr. Robert P. Miles
4532 W. Kennedy Blvd. #275
Tampa, FL 33609-2042

Dear Mr. Miles:

Thanks for your nice letter. By coincidence, just this weekend I saw your 101 reasons on the "Fool" bulletin board. You seem to be getting quite a bit of favorable comment from other viewers.

Anything you write about Berkshire Hathaway will be fine; you clearly understand the company well. I will be glad to sign your "101 Reasons," but I'm not sure if we'll be able to connect at the mall. It's likely to be a mob scene this year. I will be doing a lot of signing at the ballpark on Saturday night, but again the lines could be really long, and I won't be able to get to everybody during the game. Maybe the best bet is for you to send me a copy and I'll be delighted to sign it.

I wish you well — even *really* well! — with your project.

Best regards.

Sincerely,

Warren E. Buffett

WEB/db

Figure I.1   Letter from the Chairman

Introduction

Welcome to the World's Greatest Investment: Berkshire Hathaway

The following is a list of "101 Reasons To Own Berkshire Hathaway". The keyword is 'own.' Why? Because investors undervalue the concept of ownership. With Berkshire, it's paramount. Reasons to own Berkshire are endless, but certainly not new. What is new is the experience I bring to the table after nearly three decades in the field, and most important, a rich perspective under the Berkshire philosophy.

"101" represents a typical beginning college course. My financial education started when I first read about Berkshire Hathaway, and this list represents my years of financial education, literacy, and aptitude. Discovering Berkshire Hathaway is the end of a long journey. It is also the beginning.

Purchasing a modest hundred shares of BRK.A 30 years ago would have cost less than $1000—and would be worth over $7 million today. Consider this book a $7 million financial lesson. Even if you don't own Berkshire, the ideas expressed here could be a guideline when choosing to own another investment.

No matter what your age, you never retire from the investment process. You are never too young or too old to learn about a very important aspect of life. It's an area of increasing importance as one generation transfers the most wealth ever to the next generation, and it's critical to understand increasing pools of investments in self-directed IRAs, pensions, retirement, annuities, 401(k) programs, profit sharing, and maybe in the future, privately directed social security accounts.

Much is known about Warren Buffett. Less is known about his investment vehicle, Berkshire Hathaway. So let's talk about reasons to own it. Two important concepts in investing are *passive* and *active management* and it is important to understand both concepts before venturing into Berkshire.

Passive is a low cost, low tax, diversified, and simple index fund capable of beating 80 percent of private and commercial investors. Passive can reflect every form of investing from large cap, small cap, international, value, growth, total stock market, Dow stocks and NASDAQ stocks. Passive is good and simple—for everyone. Passive offers a simple comparison of investment decisions over time.

Active management is an overly sold, under-performing intangible concept. About 90 percent of active management, private and commercial, does not add value in any shape or form. Most active forms of portfolio management, including that which you consciously and unconsciously do for yourself, subtracts from value. Active management in any form that adds value is a rare talent.

As a disclaimer, I am a shareholder of Berkshire Hathaway. It's my largest holding. I am a private investor, a small businessman, and a lifelong student of investing. I am not associated with the financial industry or the financial media. Berkshire Hathaway or any of its wholly owned or partly owned businesses has never employed me. I am not a professional writer. I am not licensed to give legal, financial, investment, or tax advice. I have nothing to gain or lose if you own, trade, or merely observe Berkshire.

I first became a shareholder when the B shares were issued and at this writing have doubled my money. I have attended the annual meeting every year since I've owned the stock and will continue to attend each year. You may want to attend if you are interested in getting the best financial education. You can read transcripts but there are things you miss if you're not there: deciding if this investment fits you, networking with fellow owners, talking with operating managers, debating bus loads of Warren Wannabes, feeling the energy and excitement, shaking the hand of a legend, giving a standing ovation, listening to the wit and comedic timing of your chairman and vice chairman.

I am writing to help educate other investors. I have not been compensated in any form to write this book. The reasons stated are not entirely new but the compilation, collection, and writing are all unique to me. I first chose to write this book on the Internet at *www.fool.com* on the Berkshire Hathaway message board under the pseudonym 'simpleinvestor' so that these ideas would be thoughtfully debated and available to all free of charge. This is my gift to you and my modest gift back to Berkshire.

Unfortunately, we usually value things in direct relation to how much we have given up to get them. So my risk of giving away my thoughts for free on the Internet is that readers will not value them. Please use them, debate them, re-order them, make them an agenda item at lunch with a friend, or a discussion at your investment club. Anything you can do to make them better will be included in the next edition. Although a capitalist at heart, making money based on my observations of another's masterpiece seems opportunistic, insincere, artificial, and impossible to know for sure what's going on in someone's mind. I don't pretend to speak for Warren Buffett or Charlie Munger. My purpose has been to admire, observe, uncover, and expose pure enthusiasm and genius at work. What they have created, what they are in the process of creating, and what they will create in the future is, if anything, an incredible canvas.

I have attempted to compete against Berkshire by managing my own investments. I now leave my investing, capital allocation, market research, management motivation, acquisitions, and business valuation decisions to the best minds in the business. After reading my book, you may come to the same conclusion.

1 Historical Outperformance

Berkshire's historical outperformance has recently been documented by Goldman Sachs, hired by General Re for an opinion on the fairness of a merger with Berkshire. The total annual return on the Berkshire Hathaway Class A Common Stock (listed on the New York Stock Exchange symbol BRK.A) was 69.18, 52.11, 37.50, 34.85, 44.62, and 35.51 percent over the 1, 3, 5, 10, 15 and 20-year periods, respectively, ending June 17, 1998. These returns are after taxes, management costs and transaction fees.

As a comparison, the total annual return of the S&P Index was 23.78, 27.04, 19.81, 15.13, 13.34, and 12.92 percent over the 1, 3, 5, 10, 15 and 20-year periods, respectively, ending June 17, 1998.

In an investing environment where the S&P Index outperforms 90 percent of all mutual funds, Berkshire's historical outperformance can be restated as follows:

The annual percentage increase in the price per share of the Berkshire Class A Common Stock *exceeded* the annual percentage increase in the S&P Index by 1.5, 0.1, 11.1, 13.5, 13.8, and 17.1 percent over the 1, 3, 5, 10, 15 and 20-year periods, respectively, ending December 31, 1997.

Most money managers are envious of such unparalleled outperformance, and most competitors respond by saying that the performance has been lucky.

2 No Losses for Shareholders

L ong-term shareholders of Berkshire have never lost money. In fact, Berkshire has never posted a negative return. Can any long-term individual investor make such a claim? Can an institutional investor claim to have never lost money over the long term? A close look at the first page of Berkshire Annual report (Figure 2.1) reveals that besides never losing money, Berkshire's performance has been double digit in all years except

| Year | *Annual Percentage Change* | |
	Per Share Book Value of Berkshire	*S&P 500 with Dividends Included*
1965	23.8	10.0
1966	20.3	(11.7)
1967	11.0	30.9
1968	19.0	11.0
1969	16.2	(8.4)
1970	12.0	3.9
1971	16.4	14.6
1972	21.7	18.9
1973	4.7	(14.8)

(Continues)

Figure 2.1 **Berkshire's Corporate Performance vs. the S&P 500**

Year	Per Share Book Value of Berkshire	S&P 500 with Dividends Included
1974	5.5	(26.4)
1975	21.9	37.2
1976	59.3	23.6
1977	31.9	(7.4)
1978	24.0	6.4
1979	35.7	18.2
1980	19.3	32.3
1981	31.4	(5.0)
1982	40.0	21.4
1983	32.3	22.4
1984	13.6	6.1
1985	48.2	31.6
1986	26.1	18.6
1987	19.5	5.1
1988	20.1	16.6
1989	44.4	31.7
1990	7.4	(3.1)
1991	39.6	30.5
1992	20.3	7.6
1993	14.3	10.1
1994	13.9	1.3
1995	43.1	37.6
1996	31.8	23.0
1997	34.1	33.4
1998	48.3	28.6
1999	.5	21.0

Notes: Data are for calendar years with these exceptions: 1965 and 1966, year ended 9/30; 1967, 15 months ended 12/31. Starting in 1979, accounting rules required insurance companies to

(Continues)

Figure 2.1 *(Continued)*

value the equity securities they hold at market rather than at the lower of cost or market, which was previously the requirement. In this table, Berkshire's results through 1978 have been restated to conform to the changed rules. In all other respects, the results are calculated using the numbers originally reported.

The S&P 500 numbers are pre-tax whereas the Berkshire numbers are after-tax. If a corporation such as Berkshire were simply to have owned the S&P 500 and accrued the appropriate taxes, its results would have lagged the S&P 500 in years when that index showed a positive return, but would have exceeded the S&P in years when the index showed a negative return. Over the years, the tax costs would have caused the aggregate lag to be substantial.

Figure 2.1 *(Continued)*

four! Please note that since 1965, even a passive investment in the S&P Index (a better investment than 90 percent of all mutual funds) would have lost money in seven different years. Make that eight years if you include the S&P Index loss of 10.1 percent in year 2000.

There are two rules when investing money:

Rule #1 = Never lose money.

Rule #2 = Don't ever forget Rule #1.

Mr. Buffett has never reported an annual loss and my guess is he never will.

May I suggest you visit the company's website (www.BerkshireHathaway.com) and study the first page of Berkshire's annual report. It tells the whole story.

3 Low Cost, Almost No Cost

Fidelity Magellan charged $600 million in manager fees to manage $100 billion in assets in 1999. Low cost provider Vanguard Index 500 charged $200 million to manage $100 billion in assets in the same year. Berkshire Hathaway charged only $6 million for corporate administration to manage over $100 billion in assets in 1999.

When you compare short and long-term returns of the three investment vehicles, it becomes clear you don't always get what you pay for. When the assets of Magellan or even Vanguard Index 500 go up, so does management cost. This is not the case with Berkshire: When assets go up, costs go down.

Even if one day Berkshire becomes the largest domestic company measured by market capitalization, the chairman will still run headquarters with 12 employees, still pay himself a $100,000 salary, still live in his modest home, and still operate out of Omaha, in a simple 3700 square foot office. As with every investment, costs matter.

4 Proven Public Record

In a financial community known more for brilliant marketing than investment returns, it's great to have over 45 years of investment manager experience to look back and compare. It's an extraordinary track record.

Certainly historical returns are no guarantee of future returns, but a careful review of the past is better than a prospectus of what an unproven manager is promising to return. Most money managers can put together market-beating returns for three to five years. But who other than Warren Buffett can say they have consistently beaten the S&P over 45 years? Who else can say they have never had a negative return over 45 years? Who else can say they have beaten the S&P 41 out of 45 years?

5 Owner's Manual

All major purchases in your life come with an owner's manual—except financial investments. Berkshire Hathaway is the only stock to publish a manual for its owners. Chairman Buffett recommends that prospective "owners" read this publication before a purchase. If you agree with the manual, then buy the stock.

The manual will also help those who are considering trading Berkshire Hathaway stock. This stock is for those who intend to buy and hold. Traders and timers should pass on Berkshire stock. (See Berkshire's Owner's Manual, Appendix VIII.)

6 Unique Annual Meeting

Scheduled every spring in late April or early May, the Berkshire annual meeting is a unique event in the world of investments. Chairman Buffett calls this the "Woodstock of Capitalism". No other publicly traded company comes close to attracting such a large percentage of its shareholders to its annual meeting, a must for any serious investor. More than 15,000 investors descend onto Omaha to listen and learn from the greatest investor of all time.

After handling legal affairs in the first ten minutes, the chairman closes the meeting and opens up the floor. Shareholders can ask unedited questions from investing to the state of world affairs. Chairman Warren Buffett and vice-chairman Charlie Munger give shareholders six hours of their time and Mr. Buffett doesn't miss an opportunity for his shareholders to buy everything from Berkshire-related active wear to candy to ice cream to vacuums to jewelry. You can get a quote on your auto insurance from GEICO. Most products and services owned by Berkshire are displayed.

7 No Dividend

Berkshire is a pure long-term capital gain stock. Instead of giving part of the earnings back to the shareholders, which are taxed twice, the company reinvests all earnings and the company plans to continue to reinvest as long as the rate of return is greater by plowing the money back into growing the company. The chairman has promised to distribute earnings in the form of dividends if he cannot get a greater return through reinvestment.

Unlike other investment vehicles, the chairman has a personal reason to minimize dividends and build the capital base of the company: He and his family own 40 percent of it.

Berkshire will also buy back its own stock, which is more tax efficient, if that becomes the most attractive use of capital.

8 No Taxes

Unlike other popular forms of investing, particularly mutual funds, Berkshire Hathaway pays taxes for its shareholders. Berkshire has some of the diversification benefits of mutual funds without the tax risk. In 1998 the company paid nearly $2.7 billion in taxes on behalf of its owners. And the 30+ years' book value annual returns of 25 percent are after taxes. Note that the 30+ years of annual market price returns are 31 percent annually *after* taxes.

The company carries tax liabilities of unrealized capital gains. This may seem like an expense that will never be realized because the company never plans to sell its long-term holdings. So, the taxes on these gains will never be paid. Remember the chairman's favorite holding period is forever.

9 Chairman's Age

In the business of investing, age matters. Unlike professional sports, having a little gray hair in the money management business helps. How? Investors are all tested over time. The more time, the greater the test. Money managers also are given a chance to test and prove their theories and improve their skills. It is remarkable that the average age of new mutual fund managers is 28. Why not put your money with a seasoned proven manager 40 years the senior of the average mutual fund manager?

At an age when most senior corporate managers have been forced to retire, Berkshire's chairman continues to tap dance to work everyday. And if there's any indication of long life, it's having meaningful work that you enjoy.

When the chairman passes his estate to his wife and when she passes it to the world's largest foundation, will the managers of all the subsidiaries stop performing? Will Coke stop selling one billion servings each day? Will Gillette stop selling razor blades to two billion men every day?

Unfortunately, Chairman Buffett's age is often used as a reason to stay away from ownership in Berkshire. In fact, I think his age, wisdom, chosen management team and experience are reasons to own Berkshire.

10 Acts Like a Mutual Fund

Berkshire combines the qualities of stock ownership with the qualities of a mutual fund. Like a mutual fund, Berkshire is a diversified group of publicly traded companies researched, purchased and managed by the chairman. Like a mutual fund, an investor gets a low-cost basket of stocks along with the world's greatest investor with one purchase.

Unlike a mutual fund, a purchase of Berkshire also gets you many benefits not available from a mutual fund.

(1) The chairman sits on the board of directors of three of the top holdings.

(2) Berkshire holds a portfolio of wholly owned private businesses. These businesses are as diverse as the publicly traded security portfolio.

(3) Berkshire has over $27 billion to invest from its private insurance operations that is no cost.

(4) The cost of owning Berkshire does not compare to a low cost index fund or the average mutual fund.

(5) Berkshire does not advertise.

(6) Berkshire does not have a star rating.

(7) Berkshire's performance has consistently beaten the S&P index.

(8) Berkshire is in the position to help successful entrepreneurs cash out of their enterprises by agreeing to be acquired.

Make no mistake, Berkshire is more than a mutual fund. Often it is mistaken and compared to this group. The wholly owned operating businesses are more important than the equities. For decades, Berkshire's first choice use of capital has been to buy entire businesses.

Berkshire has 90,000 employees, would rank in the top fifty in the S&P 500 Index on operative earnings (excluding investment gains) and equities are only 25 percent of its market valuation. Berkshire acts like a mutual fund but is far more than that.

11 Unique Charity Program

Berkshire is the only publicly traded company that permits its shareholders to designate the charitable contributions. Each year the owners of the company determine in proportion to their ownership interest how much and where the charitable dollars will flow. In most, if not all other companies, the chairman/CEO determines which charities will benefit. Each year, 98 percent of all eligible shareholders participate in this charity program, contributing over $17 million to nearly 4,000 charities in 1999.

In 1999, shareholders of Class A shares were able to designate $18 per share to up to three different charities. The shareholders name the recipient, Berkshire writes the check.

This shareholder designated contribution program teaches the art and science of giving. This prepares shareholders to eventually plan their estates and think of a higher purpose than mere ownership of a money machine. Once you get in the practice of giving it becomes easier, particularly when your company makes it so simple.

Second, it permits shareholders to give back to a variety of causes: civic, cultural, economic, recreational, educational, environmental, as well as to children, churches and health care.

Most important, it rewards *long term ownership*. This program is for owners, not buyers, speculators, traders, or short term holders. To qualify you must be a registered Class A shareholder of record August 31. To qualify, shares cannot be in street name (with your broker ready to be traded in a flash). Class A shares must be registered with the Registrar in the owner's individual name, trust, corporation, partnership or estate. This program once again demonstrates the brilliance of its chairman.

12 Chairman's Letter and Plain Annual Report

This annual letter is copyrighted. It can be read online at www.berkshirehathaway.com. No other chairman's letter is sought after by most of the investment community. Buffett's writing style is witty, self-deprecating, thought-provoking and wise.

His letters have also been reassembled by Larry Cunningham in *The Essays of Warren Buffett: Lessons for Corporate America.*

His annual letters are the only investment book and advice you need.

Berkshire's annual report is as plain as it gets. There are no confusing graphs. There are no empty boasts from management, no color, low cost, no pictures, no hidden facts that require a lot of digging to find, no surprises, and no self-congratulations from management to management. There are no bad news reports or pleas for more time to fix its problems or blame about unfair competition or the world economy—just all the information you need to be an informed owner.

Berkshire once again takes the opposite approach. Its plain annual report is refreshingly forthright, honest, down home, and self-deprecating.

1. In recent years, the SEC has required public companies to begin reporting in its annual proxy statement a five year comparison graph of the stock/fund versus the S&P 500 Index as well as a comparison to the industry averages. Long before this SEC requirement, Berkshire had included just one table (chart) in its annual report—a more than three decade comparison of Berkshire's corporate performance vs the S&P 500 Index. Keeping with its conservative accounting practices, this chart is stated in percentage of book value not market price. The results would look even better if market price were used.

2. The table states Berkshire's numbers after tax, whereas the S&P 500 Index is before tax and other costs. Again the results would look better if before-tax numbers were used by Berkshire.

3. Berkshire goes farther than is required by the SEC and reports from its historical beginning when present management took over. The SEC requires the most recent five-year historical comparison. Berkshire provides 33+ years.

4. Berkshire shows its owners the relative results by year— the increase (30 years) in book value over the index versus any decrease (four years).

5. Berkshire's one and only chart is placed on the first page of the annual report.
6. A quick glance lets you know how your investment is performing under active management. Berkshire has never had a loss in per-share book value.

While untold thousands read it on the Internet, over 300,000 copies are printed and distributed. No other annual report is coveted by the investment community. One of the best favors you can do for your family and friends is to give them a current copy of Berkshire's annual report. It should be required reading in every college finance and investment class. Sometimes plain is the best.

13 Bridge over Troubled Water or Buffett's Theory of Relativity

The theory proves it is better to be a Berkshire shareholder during market declines.

If you're having trouble sleeping at night, go to the first page of the Berkshire annual report—you know the famous comparison to the S&P chart—but this time rank by the last column (relative results).

The real story is in the 3rd column where the annual book value results (after tax) are compared to the annual S&P results (before tax).

Figure 13.1 explains the results. Notice how the best relative years are when the market (S&P Index) has lost money. The biggest market declines led to 20–30 percent market outperformance and value added by Berkshire.

	in Per-Share Book Value of Berkshire (1)	in the S&P 500 with Dividends Included (2)	Relative Results (1)-(2)
Annual Percentage Change			
Year			
1977	31.9	(7.4)	39.3
1981	31.4	(5.0)	36.4
1976	59.3	23.6	35.7
1966	20.3	(11.7)	32.0
1974	5.5	(26.4)	31.9
1969	16.2	(8.4)	24.6
1998	48.3	28.6	19.7
1973	4.7	(14.8)	19.5
1982	40.0	21.4	18.6
1978	24.0	6.4	17.6
1979	35.7	18.2	17.5
1985	48.2	31.6	16.6
1987	19.5	5.1	14.4
1965	23.8	10.0	13.8
1992	20.3	7.6	12.7
1989	44.4	31.7	12.7
1994	13.9	1.3	12.6
1990	7.4	(3.1)	10.5
1983	32.3	22.4	9.9
1991	39.6	30.5	9.1
1996	31.8	23.0	8.8
1970	12.0	3.9	8.1
1968	19.0	11.0	8.0
1984	13.6	6.1	7.5

(Continues)

Figure 13.1   Berkshire's Corporate Performance vs. the S&P 500 (Ranked By Relative Results)

Year	in Per-Share Book Value of Berkshire (1)	in the S&P 500 with Dividends Included (2)	Relative Results (1)-(2)
1986	26.1	18.6	7.5
1995	43.1	37.6	5.5
1993	14.3	10.1	4.2
1988	20.1	16.6	3.5
1972	21.7	18.9	2.8
1971	16.4	14.6	1.8
1997	34.1	33.4	.7
1980	19.3	32.3	(13.0)
1975	21.9	37.2	(15.3)
1967	11.0	30.9	(19.9)
1999	.5	21.0	(20.5)

Notes: The S&P 500 numbers are pre-tax whereas the Berkshire numbers are after-tax.
Source = www.berkshirehathaway.com

Figure 13.1 *(Continued)*

Conversely, when the market has registered historically high returns (30 percent range) Berkshire has not been able to add value. It is no surprise in 1999 when the NASDAQ was up 86 percent; Berkshire had its worst performance in history.

This chart proves that you own Berkshire for the inevitable down years and to protect your investments in declining markets. It also proves that Berkshire is not a sail for investors during a favorable wind but rather a bridge over troubled water during nasty storms.

When the market declines, and we know it will someday, the value of individual stocks, mutual funds, and index funds will slide in direct proportion. Tech stocks and other highly leveraged issues trading at a multiple of sales not earnings will crash. Berkshire's price and market cap may decline as well but the $25 billion in float doesn't decline nor does its intrinsic and underlying value.

This chart proves that all Berkshire decade traders should hope for a major market decline and a technology bubble burst so what Mr. Buffett has carefully built during prosperous times can perform its magic. When the market declines Berkshire's cost free money (float) stays the same and maybe even grows. That's $25 billion buying opportunities.

Berkshire is not an investment for the 'average' investor. Berkshire is built for market declines not market booms. Mr. Buffett can't add value if the market continues to register double digit growth. But hold on to your hats when she tanks and $25 billion is reallocated into the best of the best.

This chart is merely a re-ranking of Berkshire's corporate performance based on relative results (column 3). Notice how well Berkshire added value when the market had a loss or single digit returns. Own Berkshire if you believe the market is headed for a sustained period of single digit returns. Berkshire is indeed a bridge over troubled water.

14 Buffett Discount

Most associate Berkshire with having a Buffett Premium— an inflated stock price because the world's greatest investor is running the company. My belief is that there is a Buffett Discount instead of a premium. Berkshire sells at a discount because it is thinly traded and has a very high insider ownership. Only three percent of its shareholders turnover each year and insiders own 40 percent of the company. Berkshire also sells at a discount because it has a very small stockholder group. For every thirty General Electric shareholders there is just one Berkshire owner.

Isn't it ironic that there is no media mention of an Internet premium, tech premium, or dot.com premium. Companies that have been pasted together on a hope and a prayer are valued at exorbitant multiples of sales and have had no earnings and may never have earnings. Yet a company that has consistently performed in all market conditions is unfairly labeled a manager premium.

Buffett is the most talked about investor and justifiably so, but little is known about his investing vehicle: Berkshire Hathaway. Ironically the only person to become a billionaire by investing in the stock market manages a superior publicly traded company that has been chosen by a few.

Because Berkshire is not included in the Dow or the much broader S&P 500 Index, no institutional owners need to own the stock. This also creates a Buffett Discount.

The first analyst to cover Berkshire, Alice Schroeder, of Morgan Stanley, calculates Berkshire currently selling at a 20 percent discount to intrinsic value conservatively calculated three different ways: float, book value, and earnings. The title of her January 1999 Paine Webber report is "Berkshire Hathaway: The Ultimate Conglomerate *Discount*." Her report points out several risk factors, none of which include a fictitious "Buffett Premium".

Sometimes Berkshire is mistakenly considered to be illiquid, when in fact it's very liquid, thinly traded but very large and very liquid. Institutions will one day discover that by owning Berkshire they have a better chance to outperform the S&P 500 Index.

Many believe that Berkshire is merely a hodgepodge of companies randomly assembled with no rhyme or reason. In fact, each piece of this conglomerate has been purposefully constructed to withstand the test of time and the creator's death.

There's much talk about the Buffett Premium disappearing after the chairman dies. My guess is the market will overreact and sell off only to realize that this company has been built to last. Another irony, a stock selling at a discount, will sell at a greater discount after the fellow who put it together with extraordinary vision passes on.

15 Loyal Shareholders

Only three percent of Berkshire shareholders choose to sell their stock each year. It is unprecedented to have 97 percent of the same shareholders from one annual meeting to the next. This three percent turnover compares to an average of 80 percent turnover for the NYSE average stock and a 200 percent turnover for the NASDAQ average stock.

In other words, only 20 percent of the NYSE shareholders are the same from one annual meeting to the next. The average NASDAQ company would never see the same shareholder even if they had a shareholder meeting every six months. No wonder NYSE and NASDAQ corporate managers are concerned about whisper numbers and quarter-to-quarter performance numbers.

Mr. Buffett likes a loyal shareholder group. He likes seeing the same happy faces at each annual meeting. Loyalty matters and is rare in this short-term orientation of corporate shareholders. I am happy to be a loyal shareholder. Remember Mr. Buffet's words "Don't own a stock for 10 minutes if you don't plan to own it for 10 years."

16 Owner Managed

The chairman and his family control nearly 40 percent of Berkshire. If you are a shareholder, your money will be invested like his own. Your chairman is deeply concerned about you, the owner. He has the same concerns about costs, staff, fees, salaries, taxes, long term performance, value, charity, longevity of the enterprise, capital allocation, and employee motivation. The chairman is an underpaid but powerful manager of your money. Every action he takes is always in the best interest of his shareholders.

Professional corporate managers are most concerned about their salary, options and benefits package and usually don't have the best interest of the shareholders. Professional managers are concerned about short-term profits and are rewarded on the short term. Professional managers are not owners.

There are few public companies that have owner/manager orientation. Professional mutual fund managers do not own the fund and are therefore not concerned about costs, taxes, turnover, long term performance, value, staff, and trading fees. Mutual funds are only concerned with quick performance and they advertise to attract large sums of money because they are compensated by the amount of assets under management. Hitting you with an annual tax bill because of their short term trading is of no concern to them. Also, passing along their advertising costs in hidden fees is no big deal.

Invest with a manager who has the same concerns as you; it will increase your chances of investing success. When someone is trying to sell you something, don't you want to know if they own it as well? Invest in an enterprise that is owner managed.

17 Stable Portfolio

Have you noticed that while the market is very busy, during the longest bull market in history, buying and selling billions of shares every day on the NYSE and the NASDAQ, Mr.

Buffett and Berkshire have not made one major marketable security (major investee) purchase since McDonalds's in 1996?

What was the general makeup of Berkshire's marketable security portfolio over a decade ago in 1988?

Capital Cities/ABC (Disney)
The Coca-Cola Company
Federal Home Loan Mortgage
GEICO
The Washington Post Company

Berkshire's marketable security portfolio looks about the same as it did in 1991. For almost a decade the only significant change has been the deletion of Guinness and the addition of Gillette, Wells Fargo, and American Express. Can any of us say that about our personal marketable security portfolios over the past decade?

In the meantime, all of Berkshire's significant moves of the past decade have been negotiated *purchases* of wholly owned companies. Unlike individuals and mutual funds, Berkshire doesn't make a sale (change) in order to make a purchase and it can buy the whole company.

Berkshire is buying wholly owned companies at fair prices versus a public marketplace that represents unfair inflated multiples of sales and in many cases with no demonstrated earnings or long-term change-free business environments.

Change has affected and will continue to affect every business including Berkshire. Change and business are difficult to split apart.

Change has hurt its World Book encyclopedia subsidiary. Software competition and the Internet has come along and changed that business dramatically.

Change has hurt its shoe businesses with production efficiencies greater outside the USA.

Change forced Berkshire to close its textile mills.

There's a lot of money to be made if you guess which companies will survive the changes. But unfortunately there's even more money to be lost investing in companies that don't survive change.

Investing is very much about probability and the probability is many times greater that you will lose with change than win with it.

Buying Value

Meanwhile the greatest investor of all time is busy assembling the opposite—looking for change-free products and services. Buying value. Mega deals like Gen Re a subsidiary selling insurance to insurance companies. And mini deals like, Jordan's furniture selling basically the same items your parents purchased. Timeless and classic methods of investments.

What does furniture retailing and a utility company have to do with Berkshire's overall big picture?

Furniture and the way we purchase it have been change-free. We basically sit on the same sofa and chair and sleep in the same type of bed that our great grandparents did.

Consuming refreshments, sitting in a chair and sleeping on a bed haven't changed since the beginning of civilization.

Change-Free Acquisitions

Even Berkshire's acquisitions and operating businesses are change free. Notice that half of Berkshire's Acquisition Criteria speaks specifically to change free (see Appendix XIII):

(2) Demonstrated consistent earning power (future projections are of no interest to us, nor are "turnaround" situations.

(4) Management in place (we can't supply it).

(5) Simple businesses (if there's lots of technology, we won't understand it)

And when Berkshire makes a change-free acquisition it doesn't change a thing after the purchase. This means change-free management. Change-free employees. Change-free customers. Change-free corporate structure. Change-free headquarters.

Unlike the majority of 'investors' Berkshire doesn't make a purchase whether it be a piece or the whole business with any intention of selling (change).

After a few missteps (US Air and a private corporate jet), Berkshire has managed to find a way to make money in the flight services business by buying the world's largest private jet fleet and the world's largest pilot training services company. Both companies were negotiated purchases, with no intention of changing ownership, with high barriers to entry and little competition.

Technology has lowered the costs of doing business but may not be good investments in and of themselves.

Nearly a third of Berkshire's marketable security portfolio is made up of just one stock, Coca-Cola, and not too much has changed there over the years. Just serving 1 billion beverages daily out of a possible 50 billion worldwide servings. Striving to serve 2 billion beverages a day.

At the beginning of commerce was insurance. Where ever there's risk there's a need for insurance. There are few certainties with investments and with life itself, but the one thing for certain is there will always be some type of risk and a basic need for insurance.

If you knew you had to have and to hold your investment(s) forever, would you:

a) change your investment style?
b) lengthen the evaluation time to decide if it is for you?
c) change what types of investments you would own?
d) change the number of investments?

Like its investments, Berkshire's best shareholders are change free. The same friendly happy faces from one year to the next.

Change-free investors do their excess compulsive monitoring *before* they purchase a stock not after.

Change-free investors don't need to monitor the price of a stock after it is purchased because they don't plan to change.

Change-free investors are monitor free decade traders striving to be century traders.

They take delivery of their stock certificates because it declares their long-term ownership orientation. And they want to go through some effort before changing their owner/partner status.

Business owners understand change free. They intimately know the costs of changing prices, letterhead, employees, training, locations and product lines.

Successful business owners have little interest in selling/ changing their company every 6 months or even 13 months. Yet the majority of stock market participants, both professional and individual do just that every year.

The majority of investors want to be in the pathway and timely ahead of change.

To successfully change invest you need to get an endless list of ten things right:

(1) Have a method of awareness. [scout, insider, newsletter, marketplace, friend, auto e-mail alerts, etc.]
(2) Guess the right industry.
(3) Guess the right company.
(4) Guess the right management.
(5) Be early in the development of the industry, company, and management.
(6) Correctly time your purchase.
(7) Have a network of information.[monitor]
(8) Correctly time your sale.
(9) Pay taxes if you have a gain [3 percent annual friction cost of change investing]
(10) Repeat step #1 [just like shampoo instructions]

You can't be late to the change party. Change investing is akin to selecting your future major league roster from little league players. A lot of ball needs to be played to determine who rises to the top. And the probability of survival is slim.

For every Ford mustang there's an Edsel, a Fairlane, a Torino, and a Festiva.

For every Ford Motor Company, there are thousands like Packard, Tucker, Bugati, Dusenberg, Studebaker, and Delorean.

Just in the past few years, for every Dell Computer, there are a thousand like Atari, Commodore, NBI, Wang, Prime, Data

General, and Tandem. And who knows where the computer industry and Dell will be in 10 years.

We are seduced into thinking that early investors win big gains. We read about the success stories. Its what makes the news. We never read about the thousands of mediocre stocks or failures due to investing in change.

Financial news in and of itself is about what is changing in the world of business. No change, no news.

The biggest change seducer of all is technology. It's the source of awareness, it's the provider of information, there's plenty of selection, it's changing every day, and there's a thousand different ways to invest. You can even use the very technology to invest. You can scout. Hire. Learn. Explore. Stay informed and be constantly updated. Time your entry and exit. All with tech.

Technology has lowered the initial costs of change. American Express Brokerage (a major Berkshire investee) will purchase a piece of a business for twenty five thousand dollars or more for free. Technology has eliminated the gatekeeper of buying and selling businesses. There's no stockbroker to monitor your moves, temper your excesses, and take responsibility for your losses.

Change investors like to assemble a five star portfolio by changing their losers and replacing them with winners at every opportunity.

Change-Free Investing

The greatest investor of all time teaches us to do the opposite. Invest in that which is change free to get the most accurate picture of the present value of future earnings.

Change investing is a ten-step process. Change free is just two steps. Profoundly simple yet little used method:

(1) Buy part of or the whole business that is at a good value with a predictable 10-year earnings stream.

(2) Don't change a thing.

Investors buy with the anticipation of change. More careful attention is paid *after* the purchase of the stock than before. It takes extra ordinary discipline to research and carefully follow a stock before it becomes part of the family. For change investors it's easier to buy it and then watch every price movement up, down and sideways. Constantly deciding to buy, sell, or hold.

When it comes to investments its best to stay with change free. Do your research. Make your decisions. And, like Berkshire, stick with them for at least a decade maybe for life.

18 No Tech Exposure

Berkshire is about value, of owning a diverse group of boring businesses that consistently grow over time. Mr. Buffett simply looks at a business as a stream of predictable cash payments over 10 years and values it accordingly. If he can't predict where a business will be in 10 years, he cannot value it and he doesn't invest.

That's why you won't find any technology, telephone, or Internet companies in his portfolio. At the 1998 annual meeting Buffett said that if he were teaching a college class on investing he would ask his students to value any Internet stock in 10 years. He said he would flunk any student who would give him an answer. It is nearly impossible to determine where technology will be in 10 years.

With Berkshire you are stuck with the most boring businesses. No Microsoft, Intel, Cisco, MCI, Dell. Buffett can't predict those businesses very well and doesn't see how anyone else can.

No momentum investing. No tech exposure. No exciting stocks in the news. Just value.

19 Asset Protection

Berkshire is a simple, low cost, and effective method to protect your wealth. Buy the stock, title the stock in your preferred method, take possession of the certificates and take yourself off the radar screen.

There is no monthly reporting by a brokerage statement, no dividend, no taxes, no tax return needs to be filed, and proper annual transfers have no gift tax consequences and require no tax reporting.

This is a simple legal method to protect your assets from financial planners, stockbrokers, lawyers, accountants, nosy neighbors, unwelcome family, and the IRS.

20 Reduces Investing Mistakes

One of the greatest reasons to own Berkshire is the chairman helps you to reduce your investing mistakes. You avoid the opportunity to misjudge an opportunity, to misunderstand an investment, to be overly optimistic, to buy high, to sell low, to choose the wrong asset class, to try to time the market, and to be risk adverse. You will also avoid succumbing to advertising, star ratings, Wall Street noise, momentum stocks, gurus, quick profits, new investment methods, technology, newsletters, insiders, the internet, your broker, your neighbor, your spouse.

When you are given the opportunity to manage your investments you are also given, in proportion, an equal opportunity to make mistakes. And one of the biggest mistakes is to not know what mistakes are possible: To not know what you don't know.

Investors by nature are optimistic. So are golfers. No golfer will tee off on a ball thinking the ball is headed for a hazard. Avoiding the hazards is what success is all about.

Human nature prevents us from hearing about investing mistakes from individuals or so called professional managers. We never hear about the water balls, the divots, the lost balls, the unrecorded swing and miss, the hazards.

The second biggest investing mistake is we conveniently forget to record our mistakes.

Most individual investors measure themselves in the short term and forget about the impact of taxes and trading costs. Individual investors don't want to compare themselves to a meaningful benchmark, like the S&P Index. Individual investors usually feel that they have had a pretty good year or a bad year. But to what standard is the comparison? Many individual investors don't have to be accountable to anyone but themselves and so performance measurement is very haphazard and unprofessional. Investing mistakes are rampant and unrecorded. The brokerage houses add to the mistakes by not properly reporting costs versus market price, by not measuring annual rates of return by investment decision, or by not comparing investment returns with a comparable benchmark.

Many professional money managers are even worse. They purposely deceive by hiding their mistakes. One common deception is to fold unsuccessful mutual funds into successful funds thereby hiding the poor performance. About 80 percent of professional money managers do not successfully compare to the S&P Index.

Mr. Buffett will be the first to highlight his mistakes. In fact his company, Berkshire Hathaway is named after one of his biggest investing mistakes, a textile mill in New England unable to sustain a profitable business. So the very name of the company is a constant reminder to the chairman that mistakes are easy in this investing business. The idea is to reduce investing mistakes. And when you do make them, acknowledge them, learn by them—and don't repeat them.

21 Easy Gift/Estate Transfer

Berkshire stock is about as easy, simple and low cost as any gift and estate transfer program. You simply write the transfer agent and gift shares to your favorite family member and/or charity. There is no cost to transfer. There are no complicated forms to fill out and no approval process. You pick your beneficiary and make your transfer. Or you can form a family limited partnership funded with Berkshire stock and transfer ownership each year within legal gift restrictions ($10,000 for an individual, $20,000 for a married couple jointly each year to an unlimited number of recipients). You don't have to worry about annual income tax returns because Berkshire pays no annual dividends.

One of the best gifts you can give your children and other dependents is Berkshire stock. Gifting Berkshire stock may help the recipient better understand investing and stay away from mistakes that you made before you became a shareholder.

22 Small Shareholder Group

B erkshire has approximately 300,000 representative class A (NYSE: BRK.A) and class B (NYSclass E: BRK.B) shareholders. The company had approximately 9,300 record holders of its class A common stock and 13,400 record holders of its class B common stock at March 5, 1999. Record owners included nominees holding at least 385,000 shares of class A common stock and 4,850,000 shares of class B common stock on behalf of beneficial-but-not-of-record owners. This compares to 600,000 GE shareholders and 400,000 Coke shareholders. Such a small number of shareholders allows a company to reduce its costs substantially. Berkshire saves costs in printing, mailing and distributing its quarterly earnings reports and annual report. In fact quarterly reports are delivered by the Internet unless you specifically request one by mail.

A smaller ownership base is usually a more loyal and informed group. A smaller loyal shareholder base facilitates communication from the Chairman and permits the chairman to have a long-term focus.

Many shareholders own just one share yet Berkshire is very concerned that they have the same rights as a large shareholder. At the annual meeting, no shareholder is too small to be heard. No question is screened in advance. No question is too simple. Most of the chairman's replies are spontaneously witty.

A few years ago a middle-aged woman wanted to know if she could ask a question even though she owned one share of stock. Mr. Buffett interrupted and said not to worry that between the two of us we own 50 percent of the company, so what is your question?

To better serve the small shareholder group, the chairman's letters are historically compiled and available at www. berkshirehathaway.com. The "Must Read and Understand Before-Purchase" Owner's Manual is reprinted in Appendix VIII.

23 Business Ownership and Time

You need to understand the concept of business ownership. The qualitative side. The management side. The philosophical side. The faith side. The integrity side.

What investors of Berkshire and every other publicly traded stock have to deal with is the burden of the value being constantly stated, calculated, broadcast, and printed for the world to see. And the business valuation could be high or low since others, mainly outsiders, perceive it.

When a value is put on something a decision needs to be made. When a value is placed on something in the stock pages a relative, work associate or friend may inquire as to your decision to buy, hold or sell. With major changes and swings in either direction the more phone calls you will get and the more decisions you need to make.

Fortunately for most small business owners there isn't a public value of their businesses every second, every minute, every hour, and every market day. And if there were with the constant changing of value a new decision would need to be made. It would freeze you from action.

Daily business valuations would shift attention from the real business of providing goods and services to deciding whether to sell, buy or hold. In fact the whole valuation of the business would shift from those that know best to outsiders who know least.

Ownership is a noun and a state of mind. It doesn't require action. Ownership is best sometimes with a lot of inaction.

This may be why our wise chairman said that what we own is not for sale at any price. To death do we part. This turns off the whole valuation decision. This ends all the phone calls.

A business owner who really understands business ownership would not buy a business for $25 million dollars only to sell it a week, a month or even a year later for $50 million. If he did that he would have to find another business to replace it with.

Why sell a business for twice your purchase price if one day it will pay you twice your purchase price every year? Why sell a business that will be worth one and a half billion dollars 28 years later? Why sell a business that continues to grow?

The above example is a real story of a Berkshire subsidiary. Fortunately for long-term owners of Berkshire, See's Candies has not been sold and will not be sold at any price. And fortunately for shareholders because See's is a wholly owned subsidiary, there hasn't been a constant reminder as to what the See's business is worth in the minds of the collective market. And we all know how smart the market is.

The second thing you need to know is that Berkshire is about time. Berkshire is about a target of 15 percent returns with a nice surprise when 25 percent returns are averaged for over 40 years.

Berkshire is about durable and sustainable businesses over time. Berkshire is about positioning itself to take advantage of whatever opportunity comes its way over time.

Berkshire is about making a wise acquisition and management suggesting that the integration will take a few years. Wise acquisitions and integration take time. It's about time.

Remember Don and Mildred Othmer who gave us all the prefect example of investing and time. Maybe Don and Mildred didn't know much about business ownership. Maybe they got lucky and because they were originally from Omaha they knew of Warren Buffett.

But the fact remains that they both invested $25,000 each in Berkshire in the 1960's and when recently they both died they were able to donate over $800 million in Berkshire stock to various charities. It's about time.

I have never met the Othmers but my guess is they didn't spend much time of all the things that didn't matter. They didn't second-guess the chairman. They didn't spend their time wondering if the market price was in line with the intrinsic value of the business. They didn't fool around with Internet message boards. They obviously didn't fool themselves by day trading.

The Othmers made a modest investment in business ownership. They lived below their means. They went about their lives teaching students. They left a sizeable estate to continue an impact on areas that they thought were important. They gave their investment time. They let it work for them. The Othmers go on teaching.

Berkshire is essentially understanding business ownership, time and the relationship between the two.

24 International Exposure

Berkshire gives its shareholders international exposure without most of the international risks. Mr. Buffett considers Coke and Gillette the "Inevitables" and plans to hold them forever. In fact his favorite holding period is forever. Berkshire is the largest shareholder of Coke with 200,000,000 shares and our chairman holds a seat on its board. Coke sells one billion servings everyday worldwide. Coke has been named the most recognized international trademark and the most preferred soft drink in China (1.2 billion people). 70 percent of Coke's sales and profits are outside North America.

The same goes for Gillette. The majority of its sales and profits are outside the USA. Buffett also sits on Gillette's board and likes the fact that Gillette captures 70 percent of the shaving market worldwide. And talk about another business that you can easily predict where it is going to be in 10 years. Everyday two and one-half billion men grow whiskers.

With most international investing you have additional risks like the political system, currency, local market knowledge, taxes, fees, restrictions, laws, high trading costs, geographical distances, and traditions. Mr. Buffett likes to invest internationally by investing in US based companies that successfully manage these additional international risks.

He lives here, his companies and managers are based here, he pays taxes here and he finds no compelling reason to increase his investing risk with international investments. Mr. Buffett's eye is global but his investments are local.

Why go outside your circle of competence? Learning to achieve market-beating performances in this country is hard enough. Why add to your degree of difficulty and bring additional risks to your portfolio? Mr. Buffet has said that degree of difficulty does not increase investment returns.

25 No Stock Splits

Berkshire is the only stock that will not split its shares. This accomplishes many things.

- First, it's easy to calculate your rate of return. Berkshire A traded for $7 in 1965 and closed at $71,000 at 2000 year end, so you have greater than a 30 percent return over 35 years.
- Second, stocks are generally split to encourage trading. The Wall Street marketers know that a $40 stock will trade more frequently than a $100 stock.
- Third, stock splits hide the real rate of return. It confuses the novice and blinds the individual investor.
- Fourth, stock splits drive up trading costs. One thousand shares of a $20 stock cost more than 500 shares of a $40 stock. Mr. Buffett has said that a hyperactive stock market is the pickpocket of enterprise.
- Fifth, stock splits encourage more market timers and traders. There's more than one guru out there hyping the

theory that buying a stock just before it splits and selling it after the split is a quick way to unlimited profits.

- Sixth, keeping the stock price high and the stock quantity low helps select a rare group of pre-qualified shareholders.
- Seventh, a non-split stock has been a no cost form of advertising. It becomes a self-selection stock for investors who think like owners.
- Eighth, a stock split focuses on price. Mr. Buffett wants its owners to focus on business value.
- Ninth, a stock split would downgrade the quality of its shareholders.

26 Shareholder Discounts

Berkshire Hathaway shareholders can call Berkshire's subsidiary GEICO (800-847-7536 or GEICO.COM) to get discounts offered exclusively to owners. GEICO was founded on the principle that government employees get in fewer car accidents. Hence the name, Government Employees Insurance Co.

Owners by their very nature treat possessions differently. Have you ever noticed how rental cars are driven differently than privately owned cars? Rental cars will go where no other cars dare go! The same thing applies to owners of businesses; they treat their businesses differently.

As an owner I get enjoyment out of drinking Coke and shaving with Gillette products. Mr. Buffett liked his time-share jet so much he bought the company.

More shareholder discounts are available at the Nebraska Furniture Mart in Omaha. In fact the shareholder discount is the same as the employee discount.

Why do public companies treat their employees better than their shareholders? Most retail operations have employee discounts but how many have owner discounts? My guess is that employees are more loyal to a public company than shareholders because they stay around longer.

I recommend visiting www.berkshirehathaway.com and clicking on their list of subsidiaries. This will show you how this holding company is extremely owner oriented. You'll also get a chance to support the company at the annual meeting. You'll get opportunities to buy auto insurance, Dairy Queen ice cream, Kirby vacuums, World Book encyclopedias, See's Candy, Berkshire logo merchandise, knives, shoes, jewelry, Coke, and even a share of a corporate jet. Buy some candy for your mother from See's Candy while you are at it.

This company was founded on the principle that shareholders own the company. Every other public company wishes they had such an extremely loyal ownership group. But if you're a trader, speculator, market timer, or professional money manager, you are more concerned about price and short-term profits. This group doesn't deserve shareholder discounts because they aren't owners.

27 Ownership Defined

How do you know if you are a real owner of Berkshire?

Certainly anyone owning one share of Class B (worth 1/30th the value of one share of class A) is entitled to all the benefits of ownership, including an invitation to the annual meeting and a copy of the annual report. But there is a difference between a casual ownership of Berkshire and real ownership.

Do you meet the true tests of ownership?

Test #1 = Is Berkshire your largest holding?

Test #2 = Is your Berkshire holding two times larger than your next holding?

Test #3 = Have you taken possession of your Berkshire Stock Certificates? (Unless you own Berkshire in a retirement account.)

Test #4 = Have you read the Owner's Manual and do you agree with the principles stated within?

Test #5 = Have you read the Chairman's Letters and Annual report for each year representing your ownership?

Test #6 = Have you attended the annual meeting for each year of ownership?

If you answered "yes" to all of the above you would be considered a true owner of Berkshire. No matter how large or small your total portfolio.

Often overlooked but critical to ownership is taking possession of your stock certificate. Possession means you don't plan to trade, speculate, time, margin, transfer, or be around for the short term. Certificate possession means you are not subjecting yourself to chair changing advice from the midnight voices in your head, your neighbor's whispers, your broker's phone call, CNBC commentators, newsletters, family, bulletin boards, and your barber. Possession of Berkshire stock means you are a real owner of the most owner friendly enterprise in the world.

Your broker probably doesn't want you to buy Berkshire in the first place, let alone ask for the certificates. This prevents the broker from making money both on the trading of your stock(s) and on the margin, or borrowing against your stock.

All Berkshire shareholders have certain hurdles to jump before they can proclaim true ownership. The biggest hurdle is your very own stock broker/financial planner who may not have your best interest in mind.

The Wall Street community makes frictional costs on every

transaction and any activity that takes away from those costs (certificate possession) is money out of their pockets. Wall Street doesn't really promote ownership. They promote the temporary rental of a business enterprise.

When was the last time your broker asked you if he/she could send you your stock certificates? When was the last time your financial planner attended an annual meeting to physically demonstrate ownership? When was the last time your stock broker showed you his/her ownership portfolio?

Unless and until stockholders stand up for their ownership rights we will continue to be at the mercy of a Wall Street community who is better at marketing than at managing money. And more importantly we must change our mindset from trading (stock rental) to ownership. The average NASDAQ shareholder tenure is six months. Did you know the average Berkshire shareholder has a cost basis of $100 representing staying power of over 23 years.

28 Merger/Acquisition Incentives

Few companies have the appeal that Berkshire has to acquire businesses whose owners want to sell them.

Successful entrepreneurs look for certain characteristics of an acquiring company just as carefully as an acquiring company looks at the seller. This is not a one-way deal. Both buyer and seller need to fulfill each other's objectives.

Entrepreneurs look for some of the following characteristics in a potential buyer:

(1) Does the buyer have enough money?
(2) Can the buyer be trusted?

(3) Does the buyer want to look at confidential numbers in order to compete?

(4) Will the seller be allowed to continue the business without major changes?

(5) What will happen to the loyal employees that built the business?

(6) Does the buyer have capital available to expand the business?

(7) Does the buyer have staying power?

(8) Will the business survive the death of the founder?

(9) Does the business fit into the buyer's existing business?

(10) Will there be any synergy by merging the company into a larger company to create even more value?

(11) Will the new buyer micro-manage the entrepreneur or attempt to change its unique culture thereby destroying what has been built?

(12) Is this a short-term play by the buyer to buy cheap and sell dear when market conditions change?

(13) Is the buyer wanting to get bigger just to get bigger and add to the ego of the CEO?

(14) Will the buyer strip the business of its assets?

(15) What is the true motivation of the buyer?

(16) Will the sale of the business solve the potential estate tax problems and preserve the business intact?

Berkshire has the right characteristics in place to be the perfect candidate for any entrepreneur looking to sell his or her enterprise. Most successful businesses need to evaluate the estate tax, business continuation, and estate liquidity problem so the business doesn't need to be sold at fire sale prices upon the death of the founder or principal stockholder.

Family concerns and business succession drive many entrepreneurs to sell their enterprise. Business owners sometimes want to unlock the cash value of their business without giving up control.

Berkshire has the cash, the character, the hands off attitude, loyalty, deep pockets, longevity, diversity, buy and hold mentality, and value orientation to satisfy most sellers. This company has been built to merge and acquire.

29 Investing with a Higher Purpose

Mr. Buffett's eventual goal is to leave the world's largest foundation. He is investing with a higher purpose through his vehicle called Berkshire Hathaway.

We all have different reasons for investing: to retire from a job we don't love, to educate our children, to buy a bigger house, to take an exotic vacation, greed, ego, to preserve wealth, power, stimulate our minds, or just to provide for our families.

However, once we have satisfied our material, health, and educational needs and wants, successful investors should strive to another level. Investors should redirect financial success for a better world. They should take what they have accumulated and give back, to make the world a better place in their own individual way.

Mr. Buffett willingly pays taxes. The chairman of this unique company brags about the amount of taxes it gladly sends to the IRS each year (in 1998 nearly $2.7 billion in taxes). While several top investment managers choose to live offshore but make their money onshore to avoid taxes, Mr. Buffett does it the simple way. He buys and holds; he minimizes costs and taxes; he sets a noble example; and he has created the world's largest foundation.

Berkshire has touched and will touch more charities than any other company. Maybe you read about the Othmers this past year. Professor Don Othmer and his wife, Mildred, each invested $25,000 with Mr. Buffett in the early 1960's. Their modest investment, long life and simple life-style has permitted them to donate $800 million.

A donation of $190 million was made to Polytechnic University of Brooklyn, where Othmer taught for nearly 60 years. His bequest was four times the school's entire endowment. This gift will transform this small 2,000 student university to another level. This gift represents nearly $100,000 per student.

Long Island College Hospital in Brooklyn will receive $160 million; the University of Nebraska-Lincoln, from which both graduated, will get $140 million; and the Chemical Heritage Foundation of Philadelphia is to receive $125 million. Planned Parenthood of New York City will receive $75 million. The Brooklyn Historical Society was left $16 million and the Omaha Board of Education, $12 million.

These are just two former shareholders of Berkshire Hathaway. Think of the compound effect of the rest of the 300,000 owners.

Coincidentally, Polytechnic University of Brooklyn is where Executive Jet Aviation operating manager Rich Santulli received his undergraduate and graduate degrees and taught mathematics.

30 Book Value per Share

Year end 1999, Berkshire's book value per share (assets minus liabilities divided by shares outstanding) is $37,987. Book value is what the owner gets per share if the company stops doing business and sells its assets to pay its liabilities.

Why is the book value of Berkshire so significant? The average top ten U.S. company (GE, Microsoft, Coke, Exxon, Merck, Pfizer, Wal-Mart, Intel, P&G, and Bristol Myers) has a book value of $10. So, Berkshire has five times greater book value per share than the combined book value of *all* 500 companies represented in the S&P 500 Index.

Berkshire Hathaway has greater book value per share than the combined book value of *all* the stocks on the NYSE. And probably Berkshire has greater book value per share than *all* 500 stocks on the NYSE and the NASDAQ combined.

Book value per share is a very conservative and old fashion way of evaluating a business. It's interesting that this stock is so powerful compared to the combined value of the rest of the stock market. Berkshire's chairman reports to its owners each year, not on market price, but on growth in book value per share. On average, book value has grown 25 percent annually since inception. Remarkably, book value has grown every year.

31 Equal Opportunity Investment

Ownership of Berkshire is available to everyone. If you have as little as a few thousand dollars you may invest in Berkshire. You can invest for a child, in an IRA, or even from another country. This investment does not discriminate. In fact this investment is best suited for the individual, and is run like a small partnership.

Berkshire Hathaway's chairman doesn't need 300,000 shareholders. Long ago, he could have bought out the interest of non-family members. With a reported net worth of $30 billion dollars, Mr. Buffett doesn't need partners.

Being the second richest person in America, he doesn't have to suffer fools gladly. He didn't have to reduce the price of ownership in 1996 to $1,000. By issuing class B shares listed on the New York Stock Exchange symbol BRK.B, class B shares trade approximately 1/30th the A share. For example, if BRK.A equals $60,000, class BRK.B equals $2,000.

Consider the following:

(1) Why does a man who doesn't need partners gladly open his arms and talent to welcome all?

(2) Why does a man who could have closed up shop to the public continue to operate in full public view?

(3) Why does he submit himself to media coverage when he doesn't have to?

(4) Why does he answer questions by financially uneducated strangers openly, honestly, and with great humor?

(5) Why does he treat his fellow shareholders as partners?

(6) Why doesn't he restrict his money management talent to family and friends only?

(7) Why not require a substantial investment in Berkshire to restrict access?

(8) Why disclose salary, ownership, family ownership, succession plans, foundation plans, and private matters if he doesn't have to?

(9) Why operate onshore fully taxed when competitors operate offshore in partnership form for only the wealthy to apply?

This is one extraordinary investment managed by one extraordinary manager. We should be privileged to be a fellow shareholder and come to know Mr. Buffett through his chairman's letters. We should remember that we are owners of Berkshire because Mr. Buffett wants to be an equal opportunity investment.

Everyone is invited to the wealth party. At Berkshire there is unity in diversity.

32 Joining a Winner

The way to beat Warren Buffett is to play him in anything but the stock market. Far too much time is spent competing against Berkshire and far less time is spent trying to learn and understand the underlying principles of long-term investment success.

I would gladly challenge Mr. Buffett in a foot race or play in a game of tennis with him. But, when it comes to investing and the stock market, I would rather be on his team or not play at all.

Only 10 percent of individual investors and "professional" investment managers beat the S&P 500. (It is surprising how many investors are unaware of the S&P Index as a measurement and comparison tool.) To beat the index is to be in the top 10 percent. Berkshire Hathaway is an investment that not only beats the index but beats it by an average of 17 percent every year for over 20 years. It should be noted that the index is easier to beat because one of the largest stocks, Berkshire, is not included in the index and nearly always outperforms it. Berkshire would be about 1.25 percent of the index today.

In 1998 you needed a total return of 28.6 percent to beat the index and a total return of 52.2 percent to beat Berkshire. How did you measure up?

I met a fellow at the last annual meeting who believed he was able to beat Berkshire by using technology stocks particularly Internet stocks. He thought Mr. Buffett was good but he was better. He believed Berkshire was missing greater returns by ignoring technology. Sound familiar? He told me his goal was annual returns of 40 percent, which is 20 percent better than Berkshire. I didn't ask him for his calling card.

33 Billionaire Maker

Warren Buffett is the second-richest person in America, worth $30 billion solely by investing in the stock market. If you study the Forbes list of the 400 richest people in America, you will find that Mr. Buffett is the only one listed as achieving his fortune solely from investing in the stock market.

Besides making himself rich through ownership of Berkshire, he has made others billionaires; Harold Alfond ($1.6 billion) sold Dexter shoes in 1993 for $420 million in Berkshire stock, Susan Buffett ($2.3 billion) Warren's wife, Franklin Booth ($1.2 billion) early investor and friend of Charlie Munger, and Charlie Munger ($1.2 billion) vice chairman of Berkshire. Several more of the Berkshire bunch have become billionaires this year; Malcolm Chace ($910 million) original family member of Berkshire textile mill, and Albert Ueltschi ($980 million) sold Flight Safety International for Berkshire stock.

Berkshire has made many centimillionaires as well. In Omaha alone there are at least 30 families with $100 million plus in Berkshire stock.

Berkshire would have made you a millionaire if you simply invested $10,000 17 years ago.

Berkshire would have made you a billionaire if you invested $100,000 in 1964.

The world's most successful investor continues to make wealth for all who choose to own Berkshire. Name any other money manager who is a billionaire maker.

34 Preserves Family Wealth

Berkshire is an ideal vehicle to preserve your family's wealth. Let's say you are one of the best of your chosen occupation; lawyer, accountant, doctor, entrepreneur, journalist, engineer or maybe you are a talented athlete with concentrated earnings. You love your career and you are well paid. In order to preserve what you have built over your career span, you need to pass your expertise on to a trusted family member. However, your spouse, children, and grandchildren may have absolutely no interest and/or no talent for your business. You have a choice, you can either let your earnings die when you retire or pass on, or you can find a vehicle to convert your hard work into an investment to pass on to your family.

The challenge of every successful career is to pass on it's wealth or convert it into a medium (Berkshire stock) that can be assumed by just about anyone, no matter their talents or areas of interest. Most, if not all, service professions are difficult to leverage and pass on to your loved ones. Even family owned businesses find it extremely difficult to successfully transfer to the next generation.

Even if you are lucky to have found a unique method of investing, you may have difficulty preserving its wealth generation. Why not preserve your family's wealth and convert your lifetime career earnings to Berkshire.

35 Salary and Ownership Disclosure

B erkshire fully discloses its modest salaries and ownership positions of its management. The chairman is paid a modest $100,000 in salary, equal to 33¢ per shareholder per year. He owns 35.6 percent of the company or 477,166 class A shares. His percentage ownership is down from 40.3 after the recent GenRe merger.

With over 12,000 mutual funds, an investor has no idea what the managers are getting paid and what percentage of the management company is owned by the manager. There is no disclosure. Berkshire, like all publicly held companies, must disclose manager salaries and management ownership.

I like having a manager that is on the same side of the table as the investor and is deeply concerned about costs, taxes, turnover, growth of the underlying book value, business succession, as well as management size and costs.

I like my manager to look out for my best interests. I also like low management salaries and high percentage of ownership. I particularly like managers being compensated in direct proportion to the long-term growth of my investment.

Compensation based on short term growth, advertising, star ratings, excess turnover, soft dollars, mutual fund supermarkets, attracting new investor money, with no ownership in the underlying assets, is extremely hazardous to your financial well being.

36 Highest Price

B erkshire is the first and second highest-priced stock in all equity markets worldwide. Still, you shouldn't confuse high price with over-priced. Likewise, a small price shouldn't be confused with under-priced and better value.

Being the highest price stock has created a no cost form of advertising. It has forced the stock reporting agencies and brokerages to expand their columns to accommodate this very unique stock. While there are thousands of penny stocks, there's only one $2,000 stock (Berkshire Class B) and only one $70,000 stock (Berkshire Class A).

Has it ever occurred to you why lottery tickets sell better when priced at one dollar? Lottery tickets like penny stocks purposely trick the buyer into thinking that low cost equals low risk. In fact, the opposite is true. Price is the salesperson's hook to get you to buy without fully understanding the value. The probability of hitting the lottery is equivalent to standing on the moon and trying to hit a three foot square on Planet Earth with a projectile. Mr. Buffett has said that he wouldn't buy a lottery ticket, but he would gladly accept one as a gift. This is obviously a man who understands price and value.

If low price increases sales, then high price must slow sales and force the buyer into greater research and understanding to confirm value.

As the highest price stock by a multiple of at least 700, once again Berkshire stands alone among all the rest.

37 Lowers Shareholder Expectations but Delivers Higher Returns

Berkshire is known for establishing an achievable goal to reach each year. Long term equities have returned on average 12 percent annually over a 50+ year time frame so Mr. Buffett believes he can promise a long term return that is 20 percent better than average. The Chairman has consistently promised a 15 percent annual return, but in fact, he has delivered long term (33 years) 25 percent annual return on book value and 31 percent annually on market price. Even with these historical returns, Mr. Buffett continues to state his goal of 15 percent annual growth of book value.

He is one of the few captains of industry that lowers expectations of its shareholders and all surprises are good ones. There are no whisper numbers or last minute news conferences to soften the blow of bad news. The latest attempt to under promise and over deliver is to proclaim the difficulty of managing an ever-increasing pot of money.

My belief is the same investing style that got Berkshire to

its current leadership position will be the same style that will continue to grow book value at or better than before. No matter what, Berkshire will continue to lower shareholder expectations.

38 Omaha Based

Having headquarters in Omaha helps Berkshire and its shareholders in many ways. Omaha is home to several insurance companies. The insurance laws of Nebraska are more favorable than other states. One of the biggest tangible benefits to a Nebraska insurance company is this is the only state that doesn't require insurers each year to provide a list of every common stock in their portfolio. There are many insurance investments located there. Omaha is one of the most central locations in the country and costs are lower there. There are other intangibles:

(1) The chairman was born there and has a simple life in Omaha. He has owned the same modest home just a few blocks from his small office on the same street. Mr. Buffett could walk to work.
(2) Other cities represent opposite viewpoints to the very nature of Berkshire. For example, New York, the hub of the financial world, has been built on frictional costs, guru and media noise, excessive short-term earnings and trading orientation. There aren't too many customer yachts in New York City. The West Coast has Silicon Valley representing over valuations and technology which is foreign to Berkshire.
(3) It's almost impossible to live a life of luxury and ostentation in Omaha.
(4) Omaha is small, friendly and easy to get around.

(5) Berkshire's location teaches investors that you can be located just about anywhere and be successful on Wall Street.

39 Berkshire's Relative Results as Compared to the NASDAQ

If you take Berkshire's changes in annual book value and subtract the annual rate of return of the NASDAQ, representing diverse technology, the new economy, the latest innovations, and new smaller companies, you get value added or value subtracted.

If you re-rank the chart below by the third column, relative results, you get similar correlations as the S&P 500 representing the 500 largest publicly traded domestic stocks.

Like the S&P 500 comparison provided by the company each year in the front of the annual report, Berkshire under performs in years when the NASDAQ is way over performing. Not surprisingly, in the five years that Berkshire wasn't able to add positive value versus the NASDAQ, Berkshire averaged 19.1 percent in those years and the NASDAQ averaged 44.2 percent.

More importantly during the seven years that the NASDAQ lost money, it averaged a 15.3 loss and Berkshire averaged a 13.7 positive annual return during those years representing a walloping 29 percent annual relative outperformance right when long-term investors need it most. This chart once again proves that ownership of Berkshire is best rewarded during declining markets not raging runaway momentum technology bull markets.

The law of large numbers will eventually work against Berkshire. Small companies and small numbers compound faster and large companies and large numbers are harder to multiply. As it grows larger Berkshire is more likely to average more in the neigh-

Year	*Annual Percentage Change*		
	in Per-Share Book Value of Berkshire (1)	*NASDAQ (2)*	*Relative Results (1)-(2)*
1974	5.5	(35.1)	40.6
1973	4.7	(31.1)	35.8
1981	31.4	(3.2)	34.6
1976	59.3	26.1	33.2
1990	7.4	(17.8)	25.2
1989	44.4	19.3	25.1
1984	13.6	(11.2)	24.8
1987	19.5	(5.3)	24.8
1977	31.9	7.3	24.6
1982	40.0	18.7	21.3
1986	26.1	7.4	18.7
1994	13.9	(3.2)	17.1
1985	48.2	31.4	16.8
1997	34.1	21.6	12.5
1983	32.3	19.9	12.4
1978	24.0	12.5	11.5
1996	31.8	22.7	9.1
1998	48.3	39.6	8.7
1979	35.7	28.1	7.6
1992	20.3	15.5	4.8
1988	20.1	15.4	4.7
1972	21.7	17.2	4.5
1971	16.4	12.6	3.8
1995	43.1	39.9	3.2
1993	14.3	14.7	(.4)
1975	21.9	29.8	(7.9)
1980	19.3	33.9	(14.6)

(*Continues*)

Figure 39.1   Berkshire's Corporate Performance vs. the NASDAQ (Ranked by Relative Results)

Annual Percentage Change		
Year	in Per-Share Book Value of Berkshire (1)	NASDAQ (2)	Relative Results (1)-(2)
1991 .... 39.6 .... 56.8 .... (17.2)		
1999 .... .5 .... 85.6 .... (85.1)		

Source = www.nasdaq.com
Note: Berkshire annual results are after taxes. NASDAQ results are before taxes. More bad news for NASDAQ traders in a taxable account, on average subtract an additional 3 percent per year for taxes from the NASDAQ returns to represent the impact of 200 percent annual turnover.

Figure 39.1   (Continued)

borhood of 15 percent but the same law of large numbers will work just as much if not more on the NASDAQ composite index.

Cisco in 1999 was NASDAQ's largest cap stock with a market cap of $450 billion and representing 8.5 percent of the NASDAQ 100 (100 of the largest NASDAQ stocks a.k.a. QQQ) giving the NASDAQ 100 a total market value of $5.3 trillion.

So speaking of the law of large numbers, Cisco is 5 times larger than Berkshire and the NASDAQ 100 is 60 times larger than Berkshire's $100 billion market cap.

So it is the NASDAQ that will be impacted more by the law of large numbers than Berkshire.

Law of Over Performance and Over Exposure

Besides runaway overvaluation, NASDAQ's other huge problem is the market out performance it has recently achieved. The more it out performs and the more that is written about it the more likely it will under perform.

Remember Mr. Buffett's two rules with investing. First rule: don't lose money. Second rule: don't forget the first rule.

Berkshire isn't able to add value during strong NASDAQ returns but it adds tremendous value during times of NASDAQ losses. The bigger the losses the more value added. Unfortunately for NASDAQ 'owners' and fortunately for Berkshire shareholders a quarter of the time or one out of every four years the NASDAQ fails to follow Mr. Buffett's two rules of investing.

So once again this chart proves that as much as it may go against our character it is in the best interest of long-term Berkshire shareholders for a bear market and NASDAQ losses. 1999 is not the prototypical year for Berkshire. In fact it is the opposite of what Berkshire stands for. Year 2000 when the NASDAQ lost nearly 40 percent and Berkshire's stock price gained nearly 27 percent is a more representative year.

Declining markets give Berkshire managers opportunities to acquire publicly traded and privately held companies at attractive prices all the while giving long term shareholders greater value.

40 Low Institutional Ownership

Berkshire is 12 percent owned by institutions which means 88 percent of the company is owned by individuals. This type of ownership base creates more of a partnership attitude, as well as an owner managed and an owner friendly company. Most, if not all, of the Berkshire subsidiaries are managed by shareholders thereby insuring owner representation on all levels. All major day-to-day decisions are made by a shareholder.

By comparison, other top ten companies measured by market capitalization have nearly 50 percent institutional ownership. General Electric is owned by 1075 institutions and over 100 different mutual funds. Another top ten company, Microsoft, is owner managed but has three times the institutional owners.

Berkshire is four times more likely to be owned by individuals than the S&P 500 Index and other insurance stocks. In the future, institutions will own a greater percentage. The institutions who own the stock are self-selected and generally think and behave much like the individual investors who own Berkshire.

Berkshire is adored by a few professional money managers including: Oppenheimer Capital, T. Rowe Price, Sequoia Fund, Manufacturers, GE Investments, Fidelity, Warburg Pincus, Oak Value Capital, AIG, Calpers, First Manhattan, University of California, Black Rock Financial, Morgan Stanley, JP Morgan, Legg Mason, Franklin Mutual, Wells Fargo, and Vanguard.

With low institutional ownership and interest, very few major brokerage firms have stock analyst coverage.

Low institutional ownership represents more owner loyalty, less turnover, more owner management, fewer costs, better compensation programs, more owner friendly, less outside interference and a long term focus.

41 Trumpets Investment Errors

With Berkshire, the first thing you hear about are the investment errors of the Chairman. When you read the annual report you clearly see what mistakes have been made. It's striking how quickly the errors are pointed out at Berkshire compared to any other publicly traded company and/or investment fund. Where else do you read about the mistakes of the Chairman and CEO? Most annual reports, delivered in full color with charts and graphs, explain in complete detail how wonderful the manager is and terrific the business has done under his/her care.

Certainly you would never hear about a poor investment choice in the very title of the business and/or fund.

How refreshing it is to hear about the mistakes in detail. We're the owners of the business. We can take the bad news and we want to hear about what we need to know as owners.

Perhaps, since Berkshire attracts OWNERS instead of traders, the Chairman can be very open, honest, and direct. Maybe because owners are in it for the long term that we are more concerned about the underlying value of the business and not the short-term swings of the market price.

Of all the names the Chairman could pick to name his company he deliberately picked his biggest mistake. Berkshire Hathaway was a New England textile mill that Mr. Buffett invested in that closed its doors because it was unable to sustain a profit. The very name of this enormously successful investment empire is named after a failed business. Through wise acquisitions and stock market purchases and Mr. Buffett's biggest error has become a top ten company.

This practice is so honest yet, is contrary to human nature. It is very human to rename a company after it closes its doors. How often do we see name changes after a public relations fiasco, an airplane crash, bankruptcy, and/or a merger.

A favorite trick of mutual funds is to fold a poor performing fund into a successful fund, to change its name to hide its below par performance and adopt a new identity. This is the federal witness protection program for the financial community. Berkshire could have changed its name over 20 mergers ago but chose not to.

What would the name of your company be if you had to name it after your biggest investment mistake? Would it be Momentum Investing, Day Trading, Buying the Latest Hot Mutual Fund, Buying High and Selling Low, Following My Broker's Advice, Following The Advice of a Newsletter, Hot tips on CNBC, Valueless Internet Stocks, Boston Chicken, Long Term Capital Management, Believing a Stock Guru, Listening To My Neighbor, Paying Excess Fees and Taxes, High Turnover, Owning Too Many Stocks, Tier I and Tier II Investing, Choosing the Wrong Asset Class, No Comparison Reporting, Thinking You Are Better Than An Average

Investor, Choosing the Wrong International Investment, Precious Metals, Commodities, Trading Short, or Margin Calls?

The name of my company would be "High Tech Naked Call and Put Option Trading".

42 Not Included in S&P 500 Index

B erkshire is a real anomaly once again. It is the only top ten (probably the top 500) public company not to be included in the index that measures the top 500 companies in the U.S. by market capitalization (number of shares times market price). It is the only U.S. company to acquire an existing S&P 500 company and not be included in the index. This turns out to be a brilliant move by our chairman.

Berkshire continues to be a stock for the people, not the institutions. Had Berkshire been added to the S&P Index, mutual funds would have needed to acquire $4.5 billion shares. This would have represented five percent of 1.5 million Class A shares outstanding. To put this in perspective, only three percent of the outstanding shares are traded in an entire year.

Historically, Berkshire shareholders are very hesitant to sell so there would have been a tremendous amount of upward movement on the stock if institutions bought in.

Being listed with the S&P 500 Index would give the stock a short term price increase, create more awareness and free advertising. However, it would mean less individual ownership, more turnover, pressure to be like the rest, and more of a trader base. Being included in the S&P 500 Index doesn't do a thing to the underlying intrinsic value of Berkshire. This is the rare result that you get when you have an owner in charge who is more concerned about value and less concerned about size.

Berkshire is a member of a more meaningful and little known index, the Forbes 40. The Forbes 40 (an outgrowth of the Forbes 400) tracks the 40 U.S. based public companies that contributed the most to individual wealth. Which index would you rather be part of—one that measures market size or one that measures wealth generation for stockholders?

43 No Tax Return

B erkshire offers the opportunity to avoid filing an income tax return. Here's how. If you own 100 percent Berkshire in a taxable account, to preserve and increase your wealth, it is possible to live off a percentage of your Berkshire holdings. No dividends or capital gains are distributed. All taxes are paid by the company. No income needs to be reported.

Instead of selling a portion of your Berkshire holdings for living expenses, which creates a taxable event, you could margin shares as you need them. By margining your shares, you also create a deductible expense if you do file a tax return on other income sources.

And on the day of your death the value of your Berkshire holdings are given a new cost basis, which eliminates the capital gain tax. If you lend your shares as you need them instead of selling, you will not be required to file an income tax return. You should talk with your accountant and/or tax advisor before attempting this strategy.

Note that margin accounts have never been encouraged by Berkshire; you lose your owner designated charitable contribution benefit because the margin shares are held in street name.

44 Welcomes Small Shareholder

Berkshire welcomes the small owner. In fact all of its principles favor the small individual. For as little as $2000+ you may own one share of this wonderful company, with full ownership rights including admittance to the annual meeting.

You may be a grandchild, child, teenager, just starting your career, mid-career, or even retired. Your investment vehicle may be a simple stock certificate, IRA, UGMA, corporate account, trust, partnership, or even an investment club. Everyone is welcome to the Berkshire party.

Hedge funds offer the best and brightest money management minds to a lucky few who can meet very restrictive requirements. Limited partners need to qualify often with capital requirements of one million dollars or more. Annual costs are usually one percent of the balance plus 20 percent of the growth. There's no give back if there's a loss and these funds usually have little concern for turnover and tax costs. Good luck if you want to check your balance or withdraw your hedge fund money more than on a quarterly basis. You may need further luck to even see what is in the hedge fund portfolio.

Berkshire is one of the best places for a small shareholder. Besides where else can you go to find a billionaire money manager to handle your investments for practically little or no cost? At Berkshire Hathaway if you read and agree with the Owners Manual, everyone is welcome.

45 Buy 1 Stock Get 100 Companies

As a glimpse of the wide ranging companies and businesses under the Berkshire fold, these wholly owned subsidiaries and marketable securities represent just about every letter in the alphabet. Can you name them?

Letter	Your favorite Berkshire Holding(s)
A	Credit card
B	Omaha jewelry store
C	Beverage
D	Shoe company
E	Fractional private jet
F	Simulator training
G	Auto insurance/razor
H	Jewelry store chain
I	Ice cream chain
J	New England Furniture Chain
K	Vacuum cleaner
L	Women's and nurse's shoes
M	Pressure and flow measurement
N	Furniture mart
O	Location of Headquarters
P	Steel
Q	Cutlery
R	Utah home furnishings
S	Candy
T	The nation's capital newspaper
U	Insurance subsidiary
V	Investing style
W	Encyclopedia
X	Motivating independently wealthy managers
Y	Internet discussion club
Z	Uniform company

Just because a company has an extended family tree representing almost all the letters isn't a good reason to own the stock. Some believe those companies were assembled with no purposeful order. In fact, the Chairman is like a master chess player and is several moves ahead of the rest of the market. Some believe Berkshire is five to 10 years ahead of all its competitors.

See Appendix XV for answers.

46 Wealth Measurement Index Member

B erkshire registers prominently in the Forbes 40 Financial index. As an outgrowth of its annual compilation of the 400 richest, Forbes Magazine has put together 40 public companies that have contributed the most wealth to its Forbes 400 list. This index of wealth is worth careful consideration.

The Forbes 40 had a return of 63.75 for 1998. That same year 10 percent of the list turned over with mostly technology stocks being added and deleted. Deletions included Ford, Nextel, Revlon, Republic Industries, and Schwab. Additions are Abbott, Clear Channel Communications, Danaher, Lucent, MCI World Com and Yahoo!.

No other stock represented in the Forbes 40 achieved its entranced to the wealth index by merely investing in the stock market, except for Berkshire. In year 2000 the Forbes 40 Index lost 33.5 percent while Berkshire was one of the few members that gained nearly 27 percent.

47 Indefensible Becomes Defensible

Mr. Buffett used to comment on the waste of executive jets for corporate CEOs. Then he convinced himself that he needed a private jet for time saving and convenience. Since he had to go back on all his words about the practicality of corporate jets he named Berkshire's jet "The Indefensible". During the Solomon crisis when our Chairman was asked to step in and basically save the company, he renamed the Berkshire jet "The Semi-defensible".

Because our money is his money, our chairman realized the cost savings of time sharing the jet. Berkshire began to save by becoming a member of Executive Jet. In 1998, he liked the aviation program so much, Berkshire bought the company.

So the indefensible became the very defensible. This deal would never happened if our chairman was not constantly looking for cost savings and valuable investments. Flying the corporate jet helped bring about a new awareness.

Just like the acquisition of Borsheim's helps capture the disposable jewelry dollars of its shareholders, the acquisition of Executive Jet brings about a unique synergy between private jet transportation and the largest collection of potential clients.

48 Largest Acquisition Its Best

Berkshire's acquisition of General Re will go down as one of its best ever. (You can learn more by studying the latest moves of the master chess player than trying to compete against him or attempting to second guess his next move.)

Berkshire stated six reasons for merging with GenRe:

(1) Create greater value for both shareholders.

(2) GenRe will be able to accept more reinsurance opportunities because earnings volatility will not matter.

(3) GenRe will be able to retain more of the reinsurance it writes.

(4) GenRe will be able to grow its international business with abundant capital.

(5) GenRe will be able to better manage its investments.

(6) Berkshire will increase it investment assets by $25 billion.

The brilliance of this latest and largest acquisition cannot be found in any book, newsletter, business seminar, MBA program and/or talk show. By a wide margin, the main reason Berkshire bought GenRe is float. GenRe tripled the float of Berkshire by adding $16 billion.

Some GenRe Investment Lessons:

(1) Buy one business get two. Berkshire gets the third largest reinsurance business in the world AND $25 billion in investable assets.

(2) Buy $25 billion investments for $16 billion.

(3) Fix the price of your acquisition during your June all time peak price of your stock to a ratio of .35 percent. The ratio is fixed but the price is subject to change over the next six months.

(4) Buy a S&P 500 stock with stock not included in the index thereby forcing the price of the acquisition down as current owners (institutions) sell.

(5) Make Berkshire more likely to be invited into the S&P 500 Index. More than ever it now clearly fits one industry category, property and casualty insurance.

(6) Use overpriced stock to buy under-priced stock.

(7) Make the deal tax free.

(8) Schedule the closing of the deal one day before the GenRe fourth quarter ex-dividend date saving another $44,692,500 (75,750,000 shares outstanding @ .59 scheduled quarterly dividend).

(9) Put downward pressure on Berkshire and GenRe stock by creating wash rule opportunities. In other words, sell Berkshire and simultaneously buy GenRe which guarantees you Berkshire stock sometime in the 4th quarter of 1998.

(10) Penalize non-converting factional shares by paying taxable cash and fixing the conversion price at the lowest possible price. After the merger the price of Berkshire went up but the cash value of fractional shares stayed constant.

(11) Save $178,110,000 annually in dividend pay-outs to be allocated to the best opportunity.

(12) Add $8 billion in sales, add $1.3 billion investment income, add $8 billion in shareowner equity and add $42 billion in assets to the balance sheet.

(13) Create the world's second largest company in equity capital.

There are probably more lessons to be learned when studying the great stock market master. Rather than second guess this particular merger, compete, guess his next acquisition, and/or mimic his public portfolio, why don't we learn great lessons from this phenomenal GenRe merger? It is only a matter of time before finance students study this recent GenRe merger to better understand stock market genius at work.

49 Free Use of Money

Berkshire is given a unique investment opportunity available to few other companies. Last year Berkshire has $27 billion in float (insurance premiums taken in before claims are paid out) and in the last five years has been paid to hold on to and invest this bundle of cash.

Imagine finding $27 billion to invest and not having to pay even the long term government bond rate of 6 percent which saves $1.6 billion annually in interest expenses less insurance claims paid.

The actual cost of this money is the underwriting loss or profit.

It is no longer possible to understand this company without understanding insurance. The importance of insurance is that it earns a 20 percent or higher return on equity on the business plus it provides free leverage to all its other businesses.

Berkshire can borrow for free which is something even the government can't do. This free use of money has grown at an annual rate of 32 percent. The total float tripled due to the acquisition of GenRe along with the super charged performance of GEICO.

The accounting picture looks very favorably on this free use of money. This no cost loan is carried as a liability, not an asset. The non-existent interest rate savings are not shown as an asset, income or as a cost savings.

So Berkshire has perpetual capital it can use, it usually comes at a profit, it pays no interest expense, and it carries this whole wonderful pleasant activity as a liability. Now more than ever, Berkshire is a property and casualty insurance company and an investment conglomerate powerhouse.

This is stealth investing at its best.

50 Truth in Advertising

Berkshire is extremely truthful with its advertising: It doesn't advertise. A few years back, Berkshire advertised for acquisitions and listed its criteria but had little success. Berkshire doesn't have star ratings either so there's no need to advertise ratings.

Contrast this with recent full-page ads from the leading provider of mutual funds. These ads are often deceptive, even if you read the fine print at the bottom. One recently published full page ad reads Q: How was it possible to beat the S&P 500 Index? A: Just ask some of the fund managers who did. They listed the six funds that beat the index without listing the 200 other funds that didn't.

What they failed to mention:

(1) The advertised returns don't reflect the load cost of three percent to buy into the 'market beating' funds.

(2) The short and long-term record belongs to some other previous manager(s).

(3) The annual after tax total return consequences of dividend distributions, short term capital gain distributions, and long term capital gain distributions.

(4) One of the six funds hasn't been around even five years.

(5) Only one of the six funds has beaten the S&P 500 Index over 10 years but that is before annual dividend and capital gain distributions consequences. If you factor the annual tax costs even the one fund that supposedly beat the S&P Index over ten years may not have.

(6) At least one of the funds isn't even open to new investors.

With Berkshire, you are assured of the highest truth in advertising standards. No ratings. No advertising. No boasts. Just market-beating performance. The annual returns always reflect all costs and annual tax consequences, and are conservatively stated as a percentage increase in book value not market price.

When it comes to your investments, stick with the providers of truth.

51 A New Retirement Perspective

Success to a businessman is early retirement. Success to a professional is no retirement. The love of leisure turns on many business people. The love of their craft turns on many professionals. Doing what they have been wired to do is one of the greatest satisfactions in their lives.

The love of work as an expression of what makes you tick is what keeps you young and living a life of purpose. This new retirement perspective applies to Berkshire in several ways.

- The most obvious is Mr. Buffett's love of his work. The indestructible construction of Berkshire Hathaway is his profession. In business, particularly the money management business, the artist is rewarded with an ever-increasing size of his canvas. The picture becomes larger and larger.
- History has proven that masters of a craft allowed to freely create, having all basic needs cared for, combined with a higher purpose, will live a long life. To take away their craft is to take away their life. And when they 'retire' their master painting or work of art becomes even more valuable.
- When you do what you do because you have been blessed with certain talents and abilities you are able to detect others who have the same make up. In the delicate business of negotiated purchases, our chairman needs to figure

out which business sellers are selling for the money and which are selling for estate preservation, access to capital, wanting to belong to a larger family, synergy, or simply growth. It takes one to know one.

What better proof than to have two thirds of Berkshire managers independently wealthy continuing to work hard for the enterprise. How else can you define love of work or doing what you have been wired to do?

• In the money management field we want our most successful managers to never retire.

• When you run your own show you can determine your own retirement timetable or even if you want to retire.

Berkshire gives each shareholder a new retirement perspective. It flips the retirement equation around and measures how long one can go on doing what one loves to do. It guarantees longevity. Remember Mrs. Blumkin of Berkshire subsidiary Nebraska Furniture Mart. Her legacy was to manage her operating company from an electric cart till the age of 104.

Berkshire treats its managers like its stock holdings and wholly owned subsidiaries; to death do they part. And Berkshire's antennas are on the lookout for negotiated purchases that come with a proven dedicated management teams in place a long way from the proverbial rocking chair.

Each Berkshire Owner Can Help

Once you have made your decision to own Berkshire, seeking a greater understanding doesn't do a single thing to intrinsic value or your investment return.

Instead of reviewing each investment move by Berkshire and monitoring the company's stock market price by the hour (remember the stock doesn't know you own it no matter how much you fret over it) why not help the chairman do his job?

How can each shareholder help Berkshire? Simply photocopy the half page acquisition criteria list (see Appendix XIII) and mail it to a prospective pre-qualified privately held company in your area.

Forget publicly traded companies because Berkshire already knows about them. Focus instead on private successful entrepreneurs unique to your part of the world that fit the criteria. They don't necessarily need to fit into a specific category of existing Berkshire businesses. The company is willing to look at any business as long as it meets ALL six criteria.

If your prospect is interested you can give them a copy of the owner's manual to see if their principles are outlined. Better yet treat interested qualified parties to a copy of the most recent annual report to see if Berkshire makes sense to them.

Your reward is spreading the word about Berkshire's acquisition plan worldwide, planting a seed for a future negotiated purchase, a sense of accomplishment, a stronger company, an ability to contribute, and an honorable mention in the next chairman's letter to shareholders for helping the chairman do his job that he loves.

In His Words

In a recent annual report Mr. Buffett writes, "Though working means nothing to me financially, I love doing it at Berkshire for some simple reasons: It gives me a sense of accomplishment, a freedom to act as I see fit and an opportunity to interact daily with people I like and trust. Why should our managers— accomplished artists at what they do—see things differently?"

These should be comforting words to individuals seeking to hire someone else to manage their hard-earned money. With Berkshire you are hiring a chairman and managers who don't need to charge an arm and a leg to run your businesses. They are not seeking vast riches in order to retire pre-maturely. They prosper in the same proportion that each shareholder prospers. Berkshire managers have every incentive to minimize expenses, increase profits, and maximize shareholder value.

Like an appointment to the U.S. Supreme Court, Berkshire's operating managers are appointed to run their chosen businesses as long as they wish.

Retirement as defined by Berkshire is to die with your boots on. To live a full life. To do what you've been wired to do. To develop a set of principles and never waiver even if your competitors and the younger generation think you've lost it, even after many years of proving you have it. To contribute more than you take. To live with purpose. To grow. To create. To earn. To prosper. To ignore your critics. To suffer fools gladly. To never stop learning. To challenge yourself. To do what you know best.

The new Berkshire retirement perspective: to retire is to 'retire'.

52 Unknown, Misunderstood Corporation

Most people have heard of Warren Buffett, the world's greatest investor, but relatively few have heard of Berkshire Hathaway, the world's greatest investment. Of those who have heard of Berkshire, most misunderstand it.

It is difficult to know about Berkshire and understand it, if you are not lucky enough to know someone who owns the stock. But when it comes to investing it's good to be unknown and misunderstood.

If you do what everyone else does you will get the same results as everyone else. The laws of mathematics, nature, and logic prove that in order to achieve returns greater than average you must do that which is different from everyone else.

In an advanced society where information is reflected instantly across the world and the stock market, it is practically impossible to find that which is both unknown and extraordinary. If you know about it chances are that the majority know about it. And if you understand it chances are that everyone else understands it.

Further it is difficult to find an investment that, until January 1999, wasn't followed by a single analyst or ever recommended by a single Wall Street brokerage house. Berkshire breaks every mold that Wall Street analysts use.

Berkshire proves the efficient market theory wrong. The market does indeed create opportunities because of lack of information, lack of analyst recommendations, misinterpretation, contradictions to long held theories, and general lack of awareness.

What should every investor do with an investment that is as superior and as unknown as Berkshire? Become an owner.

53 Chairman's Minimalist Life-style

At Berkshire cost and perceptions matter. Mr. Buffett goes to extreme measures to make sure he is setting the right example to fellow employees and fellow owners.

The company has no high salaries, no normal CEO benefits, no special CEO charities paid by shareholders, no extravagant offices, no stock options, no buildings named after the founder or even the company, and no fancy office furniture or equipment. Just straight-forward management.

At a recent annual meeting the Chairman needed to transport himself, his family, board of directors and a small security staff to various places around Omaha. In keeping with his minimalist life-style, he hired a simple private bus. There are no limos for Berkshire staff. All his annual meeting appearances are directly related to Berkshire ownership, except for the Omaha baseball team and Gorats steakhouse.

He lives in the same house and operates out of the same office building with a small staff of 12. Your chairman drives a used Lincoln automobile and could walk to work if he wanted. Headquarters hasn't changed one bit in spite of the acquisition of a S&P 500 company. Buffett's greatest single extravagant purchase has been a corporate jet which was quietly justified with the outright purchase of the parent company, Executive Jet. Even Dairy Queen wanted to donate dilly bars to the shareholders at the annual meeting, but was asked by the chairman to charge a small fee. All proceeds were then donated to charity.

Quarterly reports are posted on the Berkshire web site to save mailing costs. Mr. Buffett is no self-described technophobe, but uses technology whenever he can save Berkshire money. Every www.berkshirehathaway.com web visitor and annual report reader is greeted with a GEICO offer to bid on your auto insurance. Even the chairman's web greeting includes an invitation to do business with Berkshire.

When it comes to the management of your money, you should look to the Chairman and his life-style to get a quick reading on how your money will be spent.

54 Rich Balance Sheet

Berkshire has one of the best if not the best balance sheet of all publicly traded companies and privately held businesses. As of December 31, 1999, Berkshire's combined balance sheet shows $131 billion in assets. More impressive is a balance sheet item called shareholders' equity at $58 billion, which ranks top two in the world, and number one in the U.S.

Generally accepted accounting rules allow Berkshire to carry nearly $10 billion dollars as a liability it never intends to pay—deferred taxes. The balance sheet carries the cost of float as a liability when it is one of the greatest assets Berkshire has available—free money.

So if you combine shareholders equity with deferred taxes and float you have a company built better than Fort Knox. Berkshire has an AAA credit rating, the highest you can get by Moodys credit rating service. Berkshire has a better credit rating than the Country of Japan. If you wanted a company to insure your risks what would be your company of choice? Better yet, if you wanted to own a piece of a company with the world's richest balance sheet and superior shareholder equity, which company would you own?

55 Lazy Investor Approach

B erkshire is the ultimate lazy investor approach to investing.

- You don't need to know about intrinsic value, Federal Reserve moves, arbitrage, commodities, technology, mutual funds, or indices.
- You don't need to know what Berkshire owns and why it doesn't own technology. There's no need to worry about what Berkshire is buying or not buying.
- You don't have to buy and sell, short or go long, margin, leverage, option, put, or hedge.
- You don't have to know financial speak or whether your broker is putting your best interest before his own.
- You don't have to get up in the middle of the night to see how the Asian markets did.
- You don't need to post on the Berkshire Motley Fool bulletin board or check out Yahoo!—unless posting gives idle hands and minds something to do so you don't get tempted to sell Berkshire.
- You don't need to have a complicated estate plan or annual asset transfers.
- You don't have to spend any time on annual tax returns

because you won't get any 1099's from Berkshire. All the taxes are paid for you. You don't even need to pay the capital gains tax if you hold the stock. Upon your death the stock is given a brand new cost basis. So everyone can own Berkshire tax free, although not everyone can own it estate tax free.

- You don't need to spend anytime tracking your portfolio or comparing it to the averages. Performance measurement is done for you on the first page of the annual report.
- You don't need to understand insurance, float, deferred taxes, balance sheets, income statements, margin of safety, circle of competence, mergers, super cat, beverages, candy, newspapers, underwriting, aviation, or vacuum cleaners.
- You don't need to know much. You don't even have to do much, except decide where you want your owner-designated contributions to go, how and when you plan to spend your wealth and how you plan to transfer your Berkshire investment. Mr. Buffett has stated that "inactivity strikes us as intelligent behavior."

There is no relationship between hard work and return on investment. Unfortunately far too many investors think there is a positive relationship between time spent and portfolio return. Constantly checking the market prices adds no value to the stock. Unlike other worthwhile endeavors, when it comes to investing, the best approach may be the lazy (but intelligent) way.

56 Berkshire Post Buffett

Long term the greatest concern among shareholders is what happens to the company after the chairman 'retires'.

Most believe, including Mr. Buffett that the share price will go on sale upon the announcement of his 'retirement'. He goes further and recommends purchase of the stock at the time of his death. This is from a chairman who has never and will never recommend purchase of Berkshire.

I researched several companies whose founders died. I chose companies that had a strong leader, a visionary, innovator, one of a kind. Unlike Berkshire I selected companies that were named after their creator and visionary.

My first postmortem (sorry for the pun) is what happened to the stock of Wal-Mart after the death of Sam Walton. At the close of the year 1992, the year of Sam's death, Wal-Mart stock closed at $16 with 4.4 billion shares outstanding which gives Wal-Mart a market capitalization of $70 billion then.

Over the past 8 years Wal-Mart has made Sam proud and increased its stock valuation over 400%. With a close of $69 year-end 1999, its market capitalization is now worth over $300 billion. In the seven years since his 'retirement' Sam's company has gone on to achieve an average annual rate of return of 23 percent.

Disney: Then and Now

As a better example of a company's value after the founder's death I researched Walt Disney. Coincidentally Walt passed away about the same time Warren took over Berkshire in 1966.

In 1966 year-end Disney closed at $79.25 with 1,967,803 common shares outstanding for a market capitalization of $156 million then. And 33 years after Walt's death Disney closed in 1999 year-end at $29.25 with 2.083 billion shares outstanding making Walt proud with a market cap of $61 billion. This means that a post-mortem of Walt's death gives Disney nearly a 20 percent annual growth rate over the past 33 years.

Charlie Munger, Berkshire's vice chairman is right. With a 23 percent and 20 percent average annual rate of return, the Walton and Disney Foundations would have been well served if the founders' stock was not sold and diversified after 'retirement'.

Achieving a Vision Beyond the Visionary

Would Walt even recognize Disney if he were alive today? Did he have the vision to see all that it is today?

Did Walt have a vision for Disney Cruise Line, Tokyo Disneyland, Disneyland Paris, Hong Kong Disneyland, ESPN Zone, Disneyquest, Touchstone Pictures, Miramax, Theatrical Productions, Buena Vista International, Buena Vista Music Group, ABC Television, Hyperion Publishing, The Disney Store, and Go Internet and Direct Marketing?

My guess is Walt positioned the company to grow into these profitable businesses.

Just like Sam and Walt the concern for Berkshire post Buffett is greatly exaggerated.

Let's look at what Berkshire already has in place—prior to the departure of its chairman—that Disney and Wal-Mart did not.

Operating Managers

More than ever, Berkshire is the sum of its operating managers not its marketable securities.

All of the activity by senior management in this recent era of a stock market gone wild has been negotiated purchases of private businesses. The chairman has put together a top-notch team of the best managers that a business has to offer. Every time Berkshire has negotiated a purchase the criteria of having a management team in place has been met.

We are guaranteed the best operating managers because the founder and builder of the operating business have come along with the purchase. And his interests and the shareholders' interest have always been aligned because they have become owner/partners.

The operating managers also have the freedom to run their businesses under the Berkshire umbrella without the distractions of micro management by corporate, earnings management, shareholder relations, capital allocation, succession or any of the other concerns that they had before joining the Berkshire team.

Few if any other company, beside Berkshire can say that 75 percent of its operating managers are worth over $100 million in company stock. These managers have $100 million more reasons than the average operating manager of Disney and Wal-Mart at the death of its founders to continue the vision and growth.

Also these operating managers are unique in that they are continuing their vision and dream. With financial independence they could have retired long ago but instead continue to redefine a new retirement perspective. They work for the love of it and to make our chairman proud (the X-Factor).

In terms of compensating and motivating a highly motivated group, Mr. Buffett's eventual operating successor will have an easy task.

Running Berkshire post Warren will be like coaching Tiger Woods on his golf play. Kind of like advising Michelangelo on how to paint the Sistine Chapel. Or making suggestions to Bobby Fischer on his chess play. The best thing a successor can do is let the Mozart operating managers continue to create their own music.

Financial Capital and Strength

According to the Director of Investor Relations Jo Anna Morris of General Electric, there are only eight companies in the World with a triple A financial rating. With a better credit rating than the Country of Japan and its goal to build Fort Knox, Berkshire is one of eight companies positioned for extraordinary growth with or without its current chairman.

Credit ratings don't change after a chairman retires.

The Operating Businesses

With Re-Insurance, Passenger car insurance, flight services, furniture and home furnishings, utilities, and diversified manufacturing, Berkshire is posed for tremendous future growth. GenRe will help us become a global franchise. GEICO has all of its growth and profit ahead of it. Executive Jet already dominates the US supply of fractional jet ownership and will soon dominate the rest of the world. Flight Safety International will continue to expand, as the world demand for safe transportation is a never-ending quest. We are just starting to expand the home furnishing business with unlimited growth way past the retirement of our chief architect. We just placed our toe in the water for utility expansion in partnership with one of the best business minds (Walter Scott) with the recent purchase of Mid American.

And all the other wonderful businesses under the umbrella with a variety of annual growth rates all will add to the continuing enterprise known as Berkshire Hathaway.

See's Candies will add $60 million in earnings on $79 million in assets. Buffalo News will add $50 million in earnings on just $29 million in assets. Borsheims and Helzberg will add $40 million on $234 million in assets. Scott Fetzer will contribute $140 million in profits on $240 million in assets. Dairy Queen will add $60 million on assets of $200 million. Even the shoe group will add $35 million on $336 million in assets.

All total the other wonderful businesses listed just above will add $900 million in profits on just $3 billion in assets. This is a wonderful 30 percent return on assets. All under the direction of some wonderful operating managers.

The Marketable Securities

Representing just a third of the overall market capitalization of Berkshire's marketable securities, like Coke and Gillette will represent less importance post Buffett than currently.

All of the new allocation of capital recently has been negotiated purchases not marketable securities. Berkshire's marketable security selections are designed just like the operating businesses. They aren't for sale at any price. And the general composition of the security holdings has remained constant for nearly a decade.

Berkshire's Washington Post investment returns 100 percent of its purchase price in the form of dividends each year now.

Mr. Buffett's stock selections are cumulative in nature. Just like his operating manager successor, his capital allocation successor will have an easy job regarding the decisions of current holdings. Keep them forever and worry about allocating new cash as the operating companies send it to Omaha.

Unlike the wholly owned operating subsidiaries, Berkshire's marketable securities don't require day to day management.

Berkshire post Buffett will continue to have a board representative on all the public holdings within its portfolio, but will continue to let the built-in management of these world class companies manage themselves. Occasionally the successor will need to step in to suggest a new course of action.

Acquirer of Choice

Unlike Wal-Mart and Disney, the future post founder and current chairman is very rosy. The first stop on any potential merger candidate list is now and will be Berkshire.

Any acquisition shopper will go to where the money is and with the largest net worth of any diversified insurance conglomerate, Omaha will get the first call.

Horizontal Organization

With nearly all of its employees and operating managers outside of headquarters there isn't a company past present or future that is more horizontally structured. This properly positions Berkshire for the smooth transition from current to future management.

The Company's Name

Speaking of post-mortems, Berkshire Hathaway could have renamed itself over 100 acquisitions ago but instead continues the tradition of being reminded of the only wholly owned business (Berkshire Textile Mills) it purchased and later shut down because it was unable to sustain a profit.

The banner name will always remind future operating managers that mistakes happen and invest with a vision of operating businesses that are change free, have a moat and franchise characteristics.

Contrary to general opinion, Berkshire is not about its marketable securities. It's about the operating managers and companies. Mr. Buffett's genius is not identifying extraordinary stocks but in hand selecting extraordinary operating businesses for today and the future.

Our chairman has artfully built a Berkshire bridge to the past, the present and long into the future.

Once again Berkshire will not fall apart Post Warren. Like Disney and Wal-Mart it will grow (albeit at a lumpy 15 percent annually) and strengthen.

57 Never Broker Recommended

If you ever ask your broker about Berkshire you will probably get a negative response. Berkshire runs in direct contradiction to everything your broker stands for. Your stockbroker will probably say one or more of the following in response to your inquiry about Berkshire:

(1) Do you know how old Warren Buffett is?

(2) Do you realize Berkshire has been very lucky and cannot sustain its past market beating performance?

(3) What happens when Buffett dies?

(4) Do you know how much deferred taxes you will have to pay if you buy into Berkshire now?

(5) Coke and Gillette are having world wide problems, why would you want to inherit them?

(6) Berkshire is just a holding company of stocks. If you like Berkshire why don't you just buy the underlying securities?

(7) Why buy Berkshire when you can buy XYZ company and/or fund that has beaten Berkshire's performance in the past month, 6 months, year, two years, and/or three years?

(8) As Berkshire gets larger it becomes even more difficult to have market-beating performances. Do you know how large Berkshire is?

(9) None of our analysts cover Berkshire. For that matter few other major brokerage houses have a research report on this stock. Why would you want to own a stock without 'expert' consensus about purchasing it?

(10) One stock cannot offer you enough diversification. Why would you make Berkshire your largest holding?

My two best financial discoveries in the past 10 years would have never been recommended by stockbrokers: indexing and Berkshire. The irony of investment advice is the best advice is never given because it runs contrary to the income needs of the person giving the advice. It is the best thing for you but there is no economic incentive for your broker to suggest indexing and Berkshire. By their very nature indexing and Berkshire take money out of the pocket of financial 'professionals' and keep more money in the pocket of the investor.

Your broker will never recommend Berkshire. That's good. If you can be persuaded against Berkshire ownership then you really don't understand what you are buying. If you don't know the answers to the ten questions above you shouldn't own Berkshire.

If you want to know the answers to the previous questions read on.

(1) Mr. Buffett is 70 years old and despite recent surgery feels the same as when he was half his age. In the investment business, experience, wisdom, and a little gray hair are all advantages. The average new mutual fund manager is 28 years old. Who would you rather have manage your money?

(2) To the contrary, Berkshire's results can best be explained by a simple value approach to investing. Luck cannot explain away a 33+ year market beating performance. Luck is for the short term. Skill and experience are for the long term.

(3) A succession plan is in place and is well documented. Mr. Buffett has $30 billion more reasons to have a succession plan in place than any other investor in his company. There is no better person to plan for succession than the person who put together such a great enterprise. Berkshire has been built to last.

(4) There are $10 billion in deferred taxes. Berkshire likes to hold its investments forever. So the plan is to never pay unrealized taxes and continue to defer indefinitely.

(5) Coke and Gillette have short-term problems and some component of Berkshire will have a short term problem in the future. Berkshire has been built to look at the long term and weather any short term earnings hiccup.

(6) You can buy the underlying securities of Berkshire but you don't get the best parts; the wholly owned operating companies, float, cash flow, capital allocation, and talented and motivated management. The most talked about marketable securities of Berkshire's holdings only represent 25 percent of its market cap and it's decreasing in significance each year.

(7) Your broker will always be able to find a few stocks and or funds that have outperformed Berkshire in the short term. But remember these stocks and funds are in your financial 'professional's' best interest.

(8) For over three decades Berkshire has been saying that past market beating performance and sheer size will make future returns all the more difficult. But this has not been true. Berkshire's returns have been consistently superior despite its growth from an unknown to a member of the top ten U.S. based companies.

(9) Just because an analyst doesn't recommend Berkshire is no reason not to own it. If stock analysts knew what stocks to own why isn't there one in the Forbes 400 richest.

(10) Buy Berkshire and get 100 different companies. Most brokers over value the need for diversification. Maybe because diversification adds income to the broker.

Don't look for Berkshire to be recommended by your broker anytime soon. Berkshire is a stock that you need to know and understand yourself. If you don't know why you own Berkshire you shouldn't own it.

58 Life Lessons

Berkshire is more than the world's greatest investment, it's also full of lessons about life. As a fellow shareholder pointed out, most people buy the stock and then learn about Buffett and Munger. It's better to turn it around and read and learn all you can about the chairman and vice chairman and then buy Berkshire. If you buy it after careful examination you will be less likely to sell it.

Here are some of my life lessons learned since owning Berkshire:

(1) Children: Give them enough to do whatever they want but not too much so they don't do anything.

(2) Taxation: It is better to pay taxes than be at the receiving end of a government program.

(3) Work: Find a job that makes you feel like tap dancing to work. Hard work, hard work, and more hard work and then you will find a good investment.

(4) Simplicity: Live in the same house, drive a used car, keep your office manageable, choose a modest city away from Wall Street.

(5) Value investing: The two words are redundant. "What is "investing" if it is not the act of seeking value at least sufficient to justify the amount paid?"

(6) Writing style: Down home, engaging, self-deprecating, witty, profound, entertaining, informative, straight forward, and honest.

(7) Loyalty: Find and keep loyal shareholders. Treat them like partners. Give them owner designated charity privileges. Give shareholder discounts.

(8) Integrity: Play within the rules. Work only with people you like, trust, and admire. You will never succeed doing a good deal with a bad person.

(9) Praise: Reward your managers with praise in the annual report and at the company meeting. Tell everyone how brilliant your founder/managers are.

(10) Motivation: Berkshire is the art of motivating financially independent managers who are self-motivated. Two thirds of Berkshire's managers are worth over $100 million.

(11) Patience: Berkshire believes in waiting for the right investment opportunity even if it has to wait for decades.

(12) Inactivity: Strikes Berkshire management as intelligent behavior.

(13) Written Goals: By having written acquisition goals you attract viable candidates from all sources.

(14) Mistakes: Study your mistakes. Obsess over them. Proclaim them loud and clear. Name your company after your biggest investing mistake.

(15) Turn off the Market: Look at investing as buying a piece of a business or the whole business. The market is manic depressive, subject to wild swings in emotion and valuations.

(16) Life Long Investing: Investing is not something you do only part of your life. It's something you do for your whole life.

(17) What Not to Do: Berkshire's life lessons also include many things not to do—like, stock splitting, day trading, short term trading, timing the market, and cigar butt investing. Only own a stock for ten minutes that you would also own for ten years. Investment friction costs matter. Making more than twenty investment moves in a lifetime.

(18) Human Nature: Investing is about the study of human nature.

(19) Competition: The secret of success is to have weak competition.

(20) Concentration: Most investors overestimate the importance of diversification. Diversification is a way to cover ignorance. Investment greatness comes from choosing a few widely respected companies and holding for long periods.

(21) Leverage: Take advantage of the free use of perpetual money when it comes to you at no cost.

(22) Excellence: Hiring and working with intelligent and honest people guarantees fewer mistakes.

(23) Deny Gratification: Berkshire shareholders have chosen to deny the rewards of their investment success.

(24) Born to Invest: Mr. Buffett has been wired, for whatever reason, to look ten years into the future, to properly value businesses, to buy them at a good value, to hold them in perpetuity, and to motivate talented managers.

(25) Charity: Become the world's greatest investor in order to create the world's largest foundation. Help your shareholders become more charity minded. Annually give 4,000 different charities $20 million as designated by your owners. Make corporate charity personal and local.

Not a day goes by that I don't get some life lesson from my ownership interest in Berkshire.

59 Add Zero Every Eight and One-half Years

Berkshire has been compounding at a rate of 31 percent annually for over 30 years, which means long term shareholders have been able to add a zero to their holdings every 8½ years. So if you had $100,000 in Berkshire, you would have $1,000,000 in value 8½ years later.

Although past performance is no guarantee of future results, I would argue that Berkshire is getting bigger as it gets better. Even at a 25 percent annual growth rate you can add a zero to your Berkshire holdings every 10⅓ years. At 20 percent growth add a zero every 12½ years. At a company stated growth rate of 15 percent Berkshire becomes a ten bagger every 16½ years.

Long term compounded growth is achieved with no dividends, no taxes, no transaction costs, no 12b fees, and no annual fees no matter what the underlying performance—just a no cost way for the world's best investor to manage your money just like it was his.

60 Bear Market Tank

Berkshire is better prepared for a declining market than most, if not all, stocks and mutual funds. In fact most long term Berkshire shareholders should hope for a bear market.

When the market turns down Berkshire's price, will decline but so will every other security and equity mutual fund. Mutual funds will have net redemptions and will be forced to sell portfolio companies at fire sale prices. Highly leveraged stocks, like technology and Internet, will decline more rapidly than the overall market.

Berkshire is 16 percent less volatile than the S&P 500 Index and 25 to 50 percent less volatile than the top 10 companies measured by market capitalization. If the stock market declined 30 percent, Berkshire's shareholders equity would only decline 12.8 percent.

Berkshire will be sitting comfortably with $27 billion in float ready to deploy its resources on a prime list of bargains. Loyal and long-term shareholders will stay with Berkshire and prevent the stock from declining greater than the market. Berkshire does not need to sell any marketable securities to meet any cash demands during a market decline.

Cash flow will continue as usual at Berkshire during a bear market and shareholder loyalty will be proudly displayed. With a mere 3 percent annual turnover, stock trading will not deviate much. Besides long term shareholders are not going to mind a 50 percent drop in the price and would be advised against selling and having to pay all those capital gain taxes.

Berkshire is built like a bear market tank because it has the incredible armor of financial soundness to shield itself from attack, combined with an enormous cannon to blast away at any bargains during market declines. Short term Berkshire shareholders are always concerned about short term price movements in the stock, but long term owners should hope for a long sustaining bear market. Mr. Buffett has said that long term buyers of stock should hope for a market decline that would make stocks cheaper, just like falling hamburger prices favor a long term consumer of hamburger.

It may seem strange but market over exuberance, run away Internet stock pricing, day trading, market gurus, excessive trading, and sheer market folly are all good things for Berkshire. In the short term, marketable securities are bid too high to be attractive to management, but in the long term bargains will evidence themselves and Berkshire will pounce.

You should own Berkshire for the inevitable bear markets as well as the extraordinary bull market returns.

61 Creative Trust Management

B erkshire provides a new modern and creative trust management opportunity. This is a new concept in trust administration that may not be familiar to you but should prompt some lively discussion with your personal trust and estate attorney.

Typically, a trust is designed to provide income to a surviving spouse and then principal to the surviving children. Berkshire stock can provide a unique twist to this typical trust design.

For example, a trust of $500,000 would be invested for income in bonds generating income of 5 percent less income tax as high as 40 percent and a net of 3 percent or $15,000 annually to the income beneficiary. Income investments like bonds generally do not keep pace with inflation and over the long term are risky compared to equities.

So after the income beneficiary dies the principal beneficiary (the children) are given capital that has been seriously impacted by inflation (3 percent annually). Over 10 years, $500,000 would be worth just $372,000. Over 20 years, inflation would impact $500,000 by reducing the buying power to just $277,000, nearly half.

Berkshire creative trust management maximizes current income, reduces annual taxes, and protects the purchasing power to the remaining beneficiaries.

Continuing my example, $500,000 of Berkshire stock may generate as much as $155,000 in annual capital appreciation to the surviving spouse, ten times more annually than a typical income trust. And if the trustee simply transfers shares representing the annual appreciation of the trust instead of selling the stock to generate income, there would be no capital gain tax consequences.

If the income beneficiary margins the shares that are needed for income then no capital gain taxes are due. Income taxes are deferred until death and possibly eliminated. Also, annual margin interest may be tax deductible.

Upon the death of the income beneficiary, the purchasing power of the principal beneficiaries has been preserved with Berkshire stock.

62 Margin for Life-style

Berkshire provides an excellent opportunity to margin for life-style. Mr. Buffett would never recommend margin, a 'variable' rate interest, only loan against your stock. But a margin loan can be an efficient way to reach your financial goal.

A margin loan against your appreciated Berkshire stock means you cannot participate in the owner designated charitable contribution program because your stock certificates are on loan to your broker. Also a margin loan makes your Berkshire holdings subject to a margin call if the stock price falls 50 percent which might trigger a taxable event. Margin loans are not available in non-taxable accounts.

Some investors have smartly chosen to beat Berkshire with Berkshire. That is buying Berkshire and margining the stock to buy more Berkshire. This aggressive strategy has paid off handsomely as Berkshire has appreciated 31 percent annually and margin rates have averaged less than 10 percent.

Certainly margining Berkshire is a better alternative than margining technology and/or Internet stocks. This investing strategy has proven to increase risks greater than the 'investor' understands. Margin on Berkshire is a far more conservative strategy for investors wanting to enhance their returns who can't stand being patient for the principal only to grow.

On the other hand margin for life-style is a method to generate current income, create a tax deductible expense, and prevent realizing capital gains. Margin for life-style is a way to personally defer taxes (just like Berkshire) and reset the cost basis of your stock upon your death.

For example, let's say you had the good fortune to invest $70,000 in Berkshire stock 8½ years ago, now have a balance of $700,000, and you want to generate $70,000 in annual income without taxes.

You simply lend one of your A shares to your broker, borrow $70,000, and pay 7 percent annually or $4,900 (or you can let the margin loan interest "accrue" against your account). You can deduct the margin interest whether you pay or accrue such interest and do not have to pay capital gains of (20 percent) $14,000. You have achieved income free of taxes and deferred taxes at the same time. Hopefully, your A share value will continue to grow by 5 percent to 15 percent more than your annual margin expense.

After your death, your A share is revalued at the time of your death with a new cost basis and your heirs then pay off your on-going margin balance. You have successfully beaten the capital gain tax while insuring your capital has kept pace with inflation. As long as you keep your margin loan never more than say 25 percent of the overall portfolio valuation, the risk of a margin call is very remote.

63 Acquirer of Choice

Omaha is the first stop for every major merger and acquisition deal. Berkshire has more than enough cash and one man makes the decision in less than five minutes, sometimes faster.

Berkshire is the only company both private and public that publishes its acquisition criteria in its annual report. There's no mystery as to what Berkshire is looking for. Their acquisition appetite is growing rapidly and is insatiable, now looking for deals in the $5 to $20 billion range.

Berkshire can afford to be very patient; it will select only from the best, usually will have first choice, and can swallow just about any boring business. Berkshire will always compare any purchase of a whole piece of a privately held business with purchasing a smaller piece of a well-regarded public business.

Additionally, Berkshire can offer cash or if the deal is right for Berkshire shareholders, a piece of Berkshire itself. The acquired company gets to become part of a collection of wonderful businesses at what may result in a tax-free exchange of stock.

A seller of a business gets to convert a stock that may need to be sold for estate tax purposes and prevent a fire sale of the business at death. The seller gets a supercharged stock in exchange and succession is guaranteed.

Another key incentive is that Berkshire removes from the seller the burden of being a public company—raising and allocating capital, dealing with shareholders, analysts, the media, dividends, annual meetings and annual reports.

Berkshire continues to list its acquisition criteria as follows:

(1) large purchase (minimum $50 million before tax earnings)
(2) consistent earnings
(3) good return of equity with little debt
(4) management remains as significant owners
(5) simple business
(6) offering price
(7) no unfriendly takeovers
(8) preference to buy for cash

Berkshire buys to keep and 75 percent of its operating managers of its wholly owned subsidiaries have a net worth greater than $100 million. It has never lost an operating manager to a competitor.

Don't you wish your business met the Berkshire criteria?

64 Despised

Berkshire is not well loved by the 'professional' money managers. Berkshire's performance is a constant reminder of what is a profession filled with mediocrity and subpar performance. Actually the money management business as a whole does not add value.

You would think that if managers charge one percent of the value of the assets each year, they would add at least two percent. Well the sad truth is that while most 'professionals' charge one percent of the value, their performance is two percentage points less than the market. What other business would get away with charging more for performing less?

The client not only pays one percent annually but is stuck with a tax bill due to excessive trading of another three percent annually. Professionals need portfolio turnover to create a smoke screen and justify their existence. As a whole the money management industry is better at self-promotion than at managing money.

Ironically, if you want to earn a greater return on your money than what Berkshire has offered, you need to enter the money management business itself.

Let's say you have $100,000 in investment assets and you want a 50 percent annual no risk guaranteed return on your money, which would easily beat Berkshire. All you need to do is find 50 'clients' with $100,000 each willing to let you manage their money for a 1 percent annual fee.

Fifty people with similar assets paying 1 percent each gives you a 50 percent return with no risk. You don't even have to invest your personal assets in the same investments that you recommend for your 'clients'. You are making your market beating returns from a money management fee not superior investment advice and strategies. And you can keep your own assets in cash and you will still get a 50 percent return compliments of your 50 clients.

Unfortunately, you need to do several things to keep your extraordinary market beating and Berkshire beating returns:

(1) You need to keep your clients in the dark. Don't educate them. The less they know the better. Emphasize the warm fuzzies.

(2) Get your clients big quick early returns so they don't want to change 'professionals' because of the tax consequences.

(3) Don't offer any comparison. You can't afford to show how no value is being added in exchange for your fee. Heaven forbid to compare your after-tax, after-fee performance to the S&P 500 Index.

(4) Make the fee seem very small. One percent of assets annually appears nominal. Quote your fee as a percent of the total portfolio, not as a percent of the earnings of the portfolio.

(5) Become your clients' friend and win their loyalty so they will feel bad if they fire you. You can fire a 'professional', but not a friend.

(6) Make your clients feel dependent so they don't have the confidence to do the money management job themselves.

(7) Use code words to create confusion and prevent financial literacy and education. Make sure the monthly statements are confusing.

(8) Keep market-beating performers quiet. Develop a momentum investing style which leads to excessive trading. Always jump off the horse that has fallen behind and jump on the horse that is leading the pack. Aggressively attack any long-term value investing and tax efficient approach.

(9) Try to get your fee paid in secret. Make sure it is deducted quarterly without the client writing a check. Have your client sign a limited Power of Attorney to allow you to withdraw the management fee quarterly from the account.

(10) Aggressively attack any market beating performers like Berkshire; suggest luck, old age, premium price, tax penalties, death, lack of succession, inability to continue market-beating level. Whatever it takes you must despise those that charge far too little and deliver far too much value in return.

Berkshire by its very existence will always be despised by an industry that preys on the uneducated and insecure customer base with no comparison offered. I used to think the government would step in to prevent this financial pick pocketing. The government would protect innocent victims from snake oil salesmen not adding value. The government would insist upon comparison reporting, no soft money compensation, no deductions from client accounts by advisors. Then I woke up and realized the government is the primary beneficiary of 'managed accounts' by three percent annually in the form of income and capital gain taxes.

Financial advisors who are compensated by transactions can never recommend Berkshire. If they did they couldn't continue to charge one percent annually. How would they add value to Berkshire once they recommended it?

It's easy to despise an investment manager who consistently beats the market averages. I would be embarrassed to be in an industry whose majority of the participants (some 90 percent) are beaten by a computer. Just look how often so called 'professionals' are beaten by randomly thrown darts.

65 Deferred Taxes

Berkshire teaches the investment community about taxes. Three important lessons:

(1) taxes matter
(2) tax costs compound
(3) deferred taxes can be carried as a phantom balance sheet liability, even if you have no intention of ever paying them.

The average taxable personal account, professionally managed account, and mutual fund account loses 3 percent annually to taxes. So the average investor is flat out losing 3 percent to tax plus another 3 percent lost to inflation every year. Just the tax losses on a $100,000 investment over 20 years equals $80,000. Said differently, if your taxable investment didn't pay 3 percent a year for 20 years you would be $80,000 richer.

So tax costs matter annually and over time. A tax dollar paid is money gone forever. And tax costs compound. 3 percent paid annually is a substantial performance weight to carry. Some investors unknowingly take on more risk to battle the tax cost of high turnover investing. Taxes are the beast of burden of momentum and short term investing.

Mr. Buffett is a very astute reader of the tax code and further teaches us that deferred taxes by design will never be paid and can be re-titled a liability subtracting nearly $10 billion off Berkshire's balance sheet. As individuals we too can defer capital gain taxes on our taxable assets by holding long term. We can defer income taxes on investments by holding non-income producing assets.

But investors on the whole are not very patient. The average NYSE stock has a new owner every 13 months. By the time the average NASDAQ company has it next annual meeting, the ownership musical chairs may have its third owner. One new NASDAQ owner every six months.

Just like too many marriages, this lack of owner loyalty has a huge price. Wall Street, your broker, and the government love taxable investment transactions. Wall Street, money managers, financial advisors and/or your broker get about two percent of your assets each year. The government gets another three percent a year in taxes. And inflation takes another three percent of your purchasing power. So the average investor has a handicap of eight percent each year and you wonder why Berkshire continues to stomp the competition. The secret to investment success is to have weak competition.

Every taxable account can choose to defer taxes. Choose Berkshire and let the company pay taxes for you. About $2000 per A share in tax was paid for you in 1998 and still provided a market beating performance of 52 percent with no current tax liability.

66 No Earnings Dilution

Berkshire doesn't believe in diluting earnings per share. A rather clandestine activity done in the dark to 'reward' top managers at the expense of the owners. Exercised stock options come out of the pockets of shareholders and dilute earnings per share. Adding more damage to the owner rip-off, according to generally accepted accounting principles, un-exercised stock options are not listed on the income statement or the balance sheet. Their impact are mandatorily disclosed in an annual report footnote. Options are usually offered to top managers and approved by the 'employee' hand-picked board of directors who are suppose to represent the best interest of the owners, not the employees.

Berkshire doesn't believe in acting in any way that is not in the best interest of its owners. So Berkshire doesn't offer restricted stock as a form of employee compensation and therefore doesn't need to dilute its earnings per share. If stock options and earnings dilution were in the best interest of its shareholders, Berkshire would do it.

Recently Disney announced that its chairman exercised $39 million in stock options, with $68 million more unexercised. This is $107 million that isn't listed as employee compensation. This is $107 million that wasn't carried on the books of Disney, not even as a liability. This $107 million will now be shown as diluted earnings, although primary earnings will be listed first and cited by the financial press. Primary earnings are not what count. Diluted earnings are the bottom line.

Furthermore, stock options put all the risk on the shareholders. Options will be exercised only if the stock goes up. So if the stock goes up, options are exercised and pressure is put on the stock to move back down when the employee sells. If the stock goes down the options may expire worthless—100 percent of the downside risk and a share of any upside.

How is that in the best interest of the shareholder? Owners of the company cannot take a tax deduction for stock options either. Tax benefits of exercised stock options flow to the employee not the shareholders.

Berkshire has been built with the best interest of the people who own the company. You won't find exercised, unexercised, or executive stock options of any kind. There's no such thing as 'diluted' earnings.

Berkshire's policy is all compensation paid to its employees, including its executive officers, be tax deductible to the corporation. In any new purchase of a business, Berkshire immediately replaces the stock option program with a cash equivalency form of compensation (e.g., General Re). General Re's reported combined underwriting ratio (insurance losses plus overhead) will be impacted a full 1 percent from correctly recognizing this compensation.

Stock options are usually a wink between the chairman and the board. Diluted earnings are to publicly traded companies, what 12b fees, quarterly management fees, and reporting before tax costs are to mutual funds. They are a form of stealth compensation and false advertising; paid without much notice and undetectable by the average owner, particularly in good times. Who really pays much attention to 'unrecognized cost of out-of-the money options' anyway? The cost that is not recognized anywhere.

The argument for stock options is usually to attract and retain talented managers. Berkshire seems to be able to attract the very best by treating both its employees AND its owners very well. Remember 75 percent of its operating managers are also each owners of $100 million of Berkshire stock.

67 Chairman's Character

Mr. Buffett's investing talent and great intellect are well documented but his character matters above all else. When it comes to hiring someone to manage your life savings, your college money, your retirement and estate, three things matter, integrity, integrity, and integrity.

When Solomon made some bad management decisions in an attempt to fix the government bond market, it put itself on the course of tremendous financial and business disaster. Guess who was called in to save this large financial institution on the brink of credibility, delinquent moral leadership, legal, and character problems?

Mr. Buffett has so much credibility that when he is rumored to be acquiring a publicly traded stock, the target company is put at ease. Berkshire doesn't believe in hostile takeovers, management changes, or green mail. Berkshire can afford to do business with anyone it wants and choose not to do business with any management or enterprise not meeting the same high standards.

A company is built by leadership, talent, intellect and character. Berkshire didn't become a most admired company several years in a row by accident. Unlike politics, character does matter, and a company takes on the character of its leader. All of the widely admired companies are a direct reflection of the chairman's character. Over time, reputation and integrity matter above all else. The chairman's character brings out the best in others as well. There's a corporate culture at Berkshire that makes employees act in such a way to make its chairman proud.

Berkshire has been built by mistakes, intellect, luck, value, brilliance, patience, hard work, minimizing taxes and costs, and never selling a wholly owned subsidiary. But above all Berkshire has been built by 'character'. Without character an enterprise will eventually fail. With character, time will prove an enterprise's superiority, admiration, and wealth. Wealth is the by-product of applied character inside capitalism.

On the other hand, bankruptcy is the result of lack of management character. A bad reputation follows no integrity and eventually leads to mediocrity.

It is always an honor to be associated with Berkshire and Mr. Buffett, whether by being acquired, a customer, a friend, a neighbor, a supplier, or just a shareholder—an option available to everyone.

68 Six Sigma

Statistically Berkshire is a six sigma event. Although luck is sometimes used to describe Berkshire, close examination, comparison, and knowledge of statistics prove against luck and for six sigma.

Sigma is the Greek letter that statisticians use to define a standard deviation from a bell curve. This term has recently been used by manufacturing companies to set a goal to strive for.

The higher the sigma, the fewer the deviations from the norm. At one sigma, two thirds of whatever is being measured falls within the curve. Two sigma encompasses about 95 percent. At six sigma you are about as close to flaw free as mere mortals can get. Six sigma presents an ideal state that anything that can be measured continually strive.

Creating a bell curve with investment managers, 90 percent fall at or below the standard set by the S&P 500 Index. Two sigma is achieved by less than 10 percent of investment managers. Of the 10 percent that beat the S&P 500 Index, the top performers (two sigma) only beat it by 1 or 2 percent. Berkshire is in a class by itself. Berkshire easily beat the index over twenty years by nearly three times; index = 12.92 percent Berkshire = 35.51 percent.*

Mr. Buffett will argue that he is not the only investor to consistently outperform. All those that do come from one town, Graham and Doddsville, embrace value investing and generally have market beating returns.

How ironic the company that is nearly flawless obsesses over its mistakes. And one sigma investment managers that are full of flaws, advertise, do media interviews, strive for star rankings, sell their money management companies for high multiples, and write books about their investing strategies without any mention of their flaws.

Choose a six sigma chairman and company as your investment manager. And sleep well.

*(Source: Goldman Sachs' GenRe merger opinion, June 1998.)

69 Decade Trader

Berkshire is the opposite of a day trader, it's a decade trader striving to be a century trader. Berkshire makes more money through inactivity than by being active. In the most recent chairman's letter, Mr. Buffett admits shareholders would have been better off last year if he had regularly snuck off to the movies during market hours. Unfortunately with investing, activity and positive results are not necessarily compatible. Most of us have to unlearn this behavior. Just talk with any former day trader.

From early in life we are taught that gains must come from work and activity. You can't lose weight without changes in your diet, exercise, and hard work. In the service industries we sell our time for an hourly rate. In the product industries we sell goods for a price. Activity brings results. Therefore it follows that you can't make investment gains without effort.

Who would ever think that inactivity is intelligent behavior in the world of investing?

Why is it that most of us are in a big hurry to record an investing profit and make a bundle of money in the stock market, when history's greatest stock picker shows us the merits of patience, loyalty, reading, inactivity, applied intelligence, and decade trading?

Mr. Buffett has long said that each investor should be given just twenty investment moves during their lifetime. Think of it as a punch card with 20 punches—once you make 20 stock picks you are 'punched out.' Just think of all the day traders who use up their twenty within twenty four hours.

Mr. Buffett has also said that you shouldn't own a stock for ten minutes if you don't plan to own it for ten years. His favorite holding period is forever. Besides decade traders gain five percent a year compounded by not paying friction costs associated with active traders (taxes, buy sell spreads, commissions, and fees).

With a decision to own Berkshire you can accomplish all of your investment objectives with just one punch on your twenty punch lifetime investment card. And with a 25 percent annual gain on book value, you can add a zero to your Berkshire holdings every decade. I wish I had discovered Berkshire on my first punch.

70 Small Headquarters

Berkshire runs a 100 billion dollar enterprise with the world's smallest head office. Some 12 employees in a 3700 square foot office in downtown Omaha, Nebraska. Berkshire's name isn't even on the building. Berkshire's headquarters is smaller than any publicly traded company and is the only company that keeps its office size and staff the same no matter how large the enterprise grows. The Berkshire office is about the size of an average company generating $1 million annually in sales.

A small office is symbolic in many ways:

- As Berkshire has grown it has continued a very horizontal organizational structure. Acquisitions of wholly owned businesses are made with the intention of keeping present management, not replacing it.
- Berkshire is not in the business of getting bigger just to get bigger and satisfy the ego of the chairman. Growth is about adding value, not size.
- To his 90,000 employees and 300,000 shareholders, Mr. Buffett sets an example of simplicity and low cost by having a small modest office.
- By having a small office and staff, less time is needed to manage. Mr. Buffett can concentrate on what he is good at: asset allocation and management motivation.

- As the business grows there are greater economies of scale to managing more assets. More capital under management doesn't mean larger headquarters, more office space, and more staff. In fact, less staff is needed as the business grows and efficiencies are created. For example, GenRe no longer needs a shareholder relations department. And the world class shareholder designated contribution program is performed by borrowing one employee across the street from National Indemnity, a Berkshire subsidiary.
- In a business where confidentiality is vital, the smaller the group the easier it is to maintain confidences.
- To buy a piece of another business doesn't require staff, office space, and in Berkshire's case, a research department.

You won't find a public relations department, an information officer, merger transition teams, investor relations department, or any of the other typical headquarter's staffing. What you will find is your legitimate correspondence answered the same day it is received.

71 Concentration

Most investors underestimate the value of a few good investment ideas. Berkshire teaches us that concentration of investments is better than diversification. Sixty-two percent of its common stock investments are concentrated in just three stocks.

Everything you read about investments and every financial 'professional' will tell you the first order of your portfolio's business is to diversify. How many times have you heard, "Don't get caught with all your eggs in one basket."?

The major problem with diversification is that by its very definition, the more you diversify the more likely you will equal the market. Diversification is ignorance. You don't know for sure which ones, which way, or when your investments are going to perform and you can't afford to lose money so you diversify.

Concentration is wisdom. You only invest in a few widely respected companies. You outperform the market because you haven't diversified your portfolio to represent the market.

Mutual funds and even index funds sell investors on the idea that one investment gives you complete diversification. Don't own one stock but rather a basket, and most financial advisors are quick to recommend a basket of mutual funds. Talk about over diversification.

Even institutions and foundations have guaranteed themselves financial mediocrity. Most foundations would have been better off by holding onto the founder's stock that created the wealth in the first place. Instead almost universally foundations have sold the original stock and therefore under-performed the market by over diversifying, over hiring of consultants, and creating all kinds of frictional cost layers. All in an attempt to do the right thing foundations, like individuals, make the wrong choices. And that includes myself.

At one point, I needed to hire an investment manager to handle my company's small retirement program. I didn't know enough and didn't want to take full responsibility of my employees' retirement savings. I hired a money manager and diversified because I lacked investment wisdom. If one money manager is good why not hire two. I diversified managers just like you might diversify mutual funds out of ignorance and concern for safety against capital losses and employee lawsuits. By having more than one money manager and more than one mutual fund, you are less likely to under-perform but at the same time you are guaranteed to never out-perform.

The whole financial community is set up to get you to diversify; more frictional costs, more research, more taxes, more paperwork, more confusion, more fancy computer programs, more proposals, more meetings, more perceived need for 'professional' guidance, less individual confidence, and less empowerment of the individual investor.

Berkshire stands alone in its permanent belief that few investments are better than a bunch. Their public record of market beating returns is proof that concentration is better than diversification.

72 Eliminates Choices

B erkshire eliminates investment choices and provides an investment silver bullet. Too many choices combined with a lack of financial education is not a good thing. Just like diversification, we are taught that choice is good. Actually the elimination of choices would be better for the average investor.

An individual investor is swamped with investment choices; 7,000 publicly traded domestic stocks, 12,000 mutual funds, international stocks, small cap, value, growth, commodities, hedge funds, money markets, annuities, 401(k), traditional IRA, Roth IRA, educational IRA, estate taxes, insurance, bonds, REIT's, sector, municipals, registered investment advisors, stock brokers, discount brokers, index funds, tax shelters, and trusts, to name a few. It seems there are no meaningful barriers to entry in the money management business except a well funded advertising campaign.

Usually, the more choices the slower the decision making time, or the greater propensity to financially procrastinate or the greater the likelihood you hire a 'professional'. Too many choices can lead to no decision because you want to make the right decision.

I am reminded of my high school summer job at Baskin Robbins. Customers would come into the store and be overwhelmed by 31 ice cream choices. Yet eventually 70 percent of all choices were chocolate, vanilla, or strawberry. More choices slowed down the decision process, and more choices did not benefit the majority of ice cream customers.

More investment choices benefit the investment industry, not the individual investor. More investment products mean more money to the advisors to help choose; more choices means more analysts and bigger research departments.

Logic would say that more choices would add more value. But more choices haven't added value just added more money to those providing the choices. It doesn't expand the pie, just who eats the biggest slice.

More choices has led to a prolific number of financial magazines, newsletters, radio and television talk shows, mutual fund rating services, stock rating services, gurus, seminars, infomercials, and books.

More choices means more information, more advertising, more data, more static, more noise and more uncertainty all of which create a greater need for interpretation.

It is amazing that millions of investors continue to choose mutual funds that do not add value. Most funds charge 1.40 percent annually to deliver two percentage points less than the market. With a general disregard for taxes, they deliver an additional three percent annual tax bill for the privilege of taking away from value. Without a proper financial education and an onslaught of slick advertising, I fell prey to mutual funds as well. I guess most of us are English majors, not math majors.

More choices are what the free world is all about and everyone should be allowed to provide choice. But choices without knowledge, facts, and education are detrimental to our financial well-being.

The natural outcome of too many choices is to buy too many financial products you don't need. Without discipline and financial aptitude, too many investment choices leads to diversification. The ultimate low cost diversification is index funds that Wall Street hates, due to market meeting performance and extreme low cost.

With a single choice to own Berkshire, shareholders have chosen to eliminate all other investment alternatives. And position themselves to easily beat the collective choices.

73 Undervalued Stock

Berkshire is consistently undervalued. Some of this is by management's own design while most is by the market place's general misunderstanding of this security.

Berkshire is one of the few companies that continually states that it wants its market price to trade in line with its intrinsic value. Historically, Berkshire's market price has traded below its intrinsic value.

One of the reasons Berkshire is undervalued is its intrinsic value is difficult to measure and until recently no major brokerage analyst has attempted to even determine its market value. Even their conservative valuation shows the stock price to be way below the projected value.

Once again, we have an accounting irony. Berkshire carries on its balance sheet its wholly owned subsidiaries at their original cost. Generally accepted accounting principles do not allow Berkshire to restate asset values of its subsidiaries on its balance sheet no matter how much the businesses have grown in value.

Continuing the accounting irony, Berkshire's income statement properly reflects the income from its wholly owned companies but does not reflect the percentage of earnings it gets from its partially owned businesses. Mr. Buffett attempts to remedy this shortcoming by publishing 'look-through' earnings, his own accounting invention that the accounting profession and the SEC is only now considering adopting.

Even the first analyst to cover Berkshire considers its market price to be undervalued. The title of the January 1999 research report reflects this belief: "Berkshire Hathaway: The Ultimate Conglomerate Discount".

The report went on to demonstrate that Berkshire is undervalued by three different methods of measurement: float, book value, and earnings. Averaging these three values, Berkshire is currently trading at a 20 percent discount. Many think of Berkshire as a 'mutual fund' (it isn't) which results in undervaluation of the stock.

More reasons why Berkshire is undervalued:

(1) unknown and under analyzed
(2) the highest stock price
(3) the lowest trading volume
(4) very high insider ownership
(5) only 3 percent annual turnover of shareholders
(6) generally misunderstood
(7) management goal to trade at or near intrinsic value
(8) the wholly owned operating companies are hard to value
(9) GenRe merger temporarily deflated the stock price to create a greater under-valuation
(10) the number of shareholders has doubled in 1998
(11) no advertising
(12) no buy/hold/sell recommendations.

Whether or not Berkshire is undervalued currently is only for short-term traders. A premium or a discount is irrelevant to a long-term owner. Even if Berkshire were overvalued, historically Berkshire will meet it goal to provide positive value to all owners directly proportional to its underlying business success during their time of ownership.

Berkshire has never failed to exceed its previous high so there has never been a bad time to become a long-term owner.

74 Chairman's Mortality

Mr. Buffett's eventual mortality is greatly overstated and leads to another widely held myth about Berkshire. The myth is not to own Berkshire because the company has been built by someone who is currently 70 years old, which is past the typical age of retirement.

Make no mistake Berkshire is better off with Mr. Buffett at the helm. But Berkshire has been built to last. When our chairman passes, GEICO will still continue to sell insurance, See's will sell candy, Flight Safety will still train pilots, and Dairy Queen will still sell ice cream.

Fortunately for Berkshire owners, Mr. Buffett doesn't plan to retire. He has said that he plans to retire five years after his death. He's tap dancing to work everyday on our behalf and he's having the time of his life. He has stated that he would work for free and if enjoyment of life has any bearing on longevity, then Mr. Buffett has many years ahead.

If anyone has an incentive to put a succession plan in place, it's our chairman. Since at some point he must leave the world's largest foundation, he must plan for the business to continue to prosper after his term as chairman expires.

Mr. Buffett has also guaranteed continuation of ownership and no Berkshire stock needs to be sold to settle any estate taxes. Sale of Berkshire stock will come from short-term traders and speculators. Mr. Buffett has never recommended Berkshire stock, but does recommend its purchase when he dies. How's that for honesty?

A drop in Berkshire's price on and soon after his passing will be caused by those who continue to misunderstand the company and underestimate the company's ability to succeed without its chief architect. Buildings do not collapse after the death of the architect. Great buildings live on and become landmarks and examples for students.

The succession plan is in place to divide his job in two—capital allocation and management motivation. The company's cost to replace Mr. Buffett will go up dramatically since it will be impossible to find two lucky managers to split his salary and do his job for $50,000 each.

The chairman's job is something he will get better at over time, not worse. The longer he has been on the job the more lessons he has learned from his mistakes, so the better his guidance in the future.

According to American Heritage magazine, the average age of the four richest men in history in today's dollars was 86 years old: John D. Rockefeller (91), Andrew Carnegie (84), Cornelius Vanderbilt (83), and John Jacob Astor (85). All four of these men were born in the last century before modern day advancements in health care. If empire building and age are related then our chairman is in very good company.

Another reason why the chairman's mortality is overstated is to look at the succession of companies that have been built by the power and genius of primarily one individual. Companies like Disney and Wal-Mart come to mind.

These companies have prospered more after the death of its founders and chairmen. Look at what Jack Welch has done with General Electric. Coke was taken to a new level by its past chairman but still continues to sell one billion servings daily after his death.

I can't tell you who the founder of Merck was but I do know that great companies don't stop being great after the death of its founder. Gillette's chairman will retire this year but Gillette will go on and continue to dominate 70 percent of the world's shaving market.

In fact the challenge of Berkshire is to continue to make Mr. Buffett proud after his death. Berkshire's destiny is to continue the great tradition of superior return on capital. If anyone can build something as extraordinary as Berkshire, trust that same person to preserve the heritage, the beliefs, the philosophies, the commitment, the passion, the uniqueness, the value, and the results.

When Mr. Buffett passes, Berkshire stock will be on sale, probably 20 percent off. If you don't already own it, you should buy it then. You won't get the architect but you'll get great buildings and a vast campus with years of expansion ahead.

75 Competence

B erkshire defines and stays within its area of competence. Despite critics who say you must be good in all areas of investing, Berkshire solidly demonstrates the rewards for keeping way inside its comfort zone.

Famed business leader Lee Iacocca once said that you make money in the business you know and lose money in the business you don't know. Berkshire's long held belief is there are many ways to win at the game of investing and it plans to win with the way it knows best.

It is amazing to hear talk about Berkshire's unwillingness to embrace technology and internet stocks. Instead of praising such rational investing behavior, the general thought is to criticize.

The consensus seems to be if you're not good at making money in technology then you're somehow not a complete investor. Just think how great the Berkshire results would be if management would have bought Dell, Intel, Microsoft, MCI, Amgen, Cisco, AOL, Lucent, Yahoo!, and Amazon instead of boring companies like GenRe, Executive Jet, Dairy Queen, Geico, Star Furniture, Kansas Bankers Surety, and FlightSafety International.

Why does it matter how extraordinary market beating returns are accomplished? Why does the investment community hold it against Berkshire for not stepping outside its circle of competence?

Technology is in the news and is not a well-kept secret, just hard to value. Technology can make our lives better. Technology is stimulation and entertainment. Technology is ever changing. Technology is the latest and greatest. Technology is the information age. Technology is today and the future. Technology makes day trading. Day trading makes technology. Technology drives technology. Tech stocks fit well into the momentum style of investing, and the financial community, along with the government, love those transaction costs.

If I were connected to the financial community, if I were a stock broker, a registered investment advisor, a stock or mutual fund rating service, an investment letter author, an investment magazine, a mutual fund manager, or a Wall Street guru, I would talk about the technology sector non-stop. It's where the action is. It's where the money is.

So it follows that you must embrace tech stocks. And it follows that if you don't get in early you will miss the boat. Logically few investments require early entry. In fact most initial public offerings are not great investments.

Buying a business after it has been developed and proven has made more money for investors than buying on a hope and a prayer. Buying a business that is out of the news and therefore possibly undervalued is always intelligent behavior.

For the most part technology is simply herd mentality and part of herd psychology is to get the master stock picker to validate your beliefs by getting Berkshire to invest outside its range of competence. If you can't get Berkshire to validate, then attack its simple investing style as senseless and archaic.

Mr. Buffett has long said that he prefers to step over one foot bars than try to be a hero and jump over seven foot bars. Greater returns are not necessarily linked to greater degrees of difficulty. He is the first to suggest that he is not good at everything and that should be respected not condemned.

Berkshire isn't competent with international stocks either. Berkshire has chosen to invest in U.S. based companies because it's located here, is two hours away from most decision makers, doesn't need to consider currency conversions, doesn't need to understand the unique political environment of each equity, pays taxes in U.S. dollars, and most importantly, is outside its investment zone.

Some in the investment community take issue with its lack of international exposure, but most point to Berkshire letting the technology world slip by. Mr. Buffett's position on technology is akin to space travel; "I applaud the effort, but will pass on the ride."

If Berkshire can't value a company it won't buy it. If an investment is outside its circle of competence, it's not interested. There are far too many intelligent choices to make than to be stuck with following the herd.

76 Quick Inoculation

You either get Berkshire in the first 10 minutes or you don't get it. It happens fast for those that are ready.

For me, it was 30 years of acquiring an investment education by doing everything else first and making every mistake. Eventually I discovered index investing on my own. This form of investing guarantees to meet the market with low costs, low turnover, and small tax consequences.

After experiencing all forms of investing I asked myself who is the best manager of money. I then read everything I could about Mr. Buffett, value investing, and Berkshire Hathaway. I got the essence of Berkshire within minutes and my experience is that those that are exposed get it right away or they just aren't interested. There's no time-delayed discovery and enlightenment.

After your Berkshire inoculation you read, ask questions, and look to find the weaknesses. You attempt to create reasons not to invest and you're on your own because everywhere you turn some 'professional' is ready to talk you out of Berkshire and into something 'better' for you.

When the B shares were issued a few years ago, I invested and took my beloved stepfather and financial confidant to the annual meeting. As a side note my mother couldn't understand why the two of us would travel all the way to Omaha to hear the music of Mr. Buffett. My stepfather didn't get Berkshire before the meeting, he didn't get it at the Borsheim's reception, it didn't hit him when he saw the small headquarters, the inconspicuous home of the chairman, the number of attendees at the meeting, the standing ovation, the chairman's and vice-chairman's candid, brilliant and witty answers for six straight hours.

He had the opportunity to purchase B shares at the original issue price of $1,000 along with me but he didn't get it. Even my enthusiasm and passion for Berkshire couldn't convince him to make more than a modest investment some two years later. Fortunately my mother trusts me and made a sizeable investment.

A few years ago I had the memorable experience of meeting Mr. Buffett at the Omaha Dairy Queen the evening before the annual meeting and said to him that my family had made a substantial investment in Berkshire, and to make sure he continued to do a good management job. He reassured me, as he took a bite of his dusty sundae, that he and his family had made a sizeable investment as well.

I have a good friend who grew up in Nebraska, works for an Omaha-based insurance company, has heard of Mr. Buffett and Berkshire, and is a very experienced investor. I have given him books about Mr. Buffett. I have invited him to join me in Omaha for the annual meeting. I have given him a copy of the annual reports and transcripts of the annual meetings. I have personally spoken to him about my enthusiasm for this company. He hasn't been inoculated. He still talks to me about Lucent, Wal-Mart, Nike, and Fortune Brands. He doesn't get Berkshire and I don't think he ever will. Another good friend bought a small amount of Berkshire just to shut me up.

My personal attorney/CPA invested 120 percent of his portfolio in Berkshire, after reading all of Buffett's writings twice. You might say he was quickly inoculated and remains "virus-free" to this day.

77 Attracts Like Minds

One of the nice perks of investing in Berkshire is all the bright diverse owners. Berkshire is like the worldwide Mensa club without having to take an IQ test. Certainly you don't have to be a Rhodes scholar or graduate in the top 10 percent of your class to qualify for Berkshire ownership.

Berkshire just seems to attract the brightest and most successful; famed owners from the business world like Bill Gates, a Nobel peace prize winning economist, and media celebrities like Martha Stewart, Tom Brokaw and Ted Koppel. Not that investments from successful smart people mean an investment is the best, it's just a common law of nature that like minds are attracted.

My personal experience writing this book on Motley Fool's (www.fool.com) Berkshire Hathaway Bulletin Board has been that very intelligent minds are brought together by this company. Doctors, lawyers, business people, retirees, investment managers, writers, dentists, students, financial analysts, accountants, housewives, and generally people serious about managing their money gather together daily to debate online.

Even Hollywood types are attracted to Berkshire. In *Smart Money* magazine (March 1998) Ben Stein, host of "Win Ben Stein's Money", a quiz show, admits to owning Berkshire Hathaway. He owned 100 shares purchased at prices from $900 to $20,000, and has since sold all but 10 shares believing that Berkshire will eventually not beat the market. Mr. Stein's choice makes some very compelling arguments to the false pursuit of picking stocks to beat the market (defined as the collective wisdom of all investors). I wonder if Mr. Stein is still happy with his decision to sell 90 percent of his holdings?

You can skip the annual meeting in May and read the transcripts, but you will miss one of the best rewards for attending; to mingle with fellow shareholders.

This is a diverse group from all different backgrounds visiting from all areas of the world. They probably have different political and religious beliefs and are at different stations in their lives. But they have been attracted to Berkshire and Omaha because they think alike when it comes to investing. Ultimately, we are defined by the company we keep.

78 Classic

Only time can make a classic and Berkshire has become one. Anyone can put together a string of market beating performances for up to five years. After five years most out-performers revert back to the median and quite a few under-perform because so much money flows to early success. Large inflows following market success usually guarantees failure.

Peter Lynch is often cited as a money master and classic. However, close examination of his investment record at Fidelity's Magellan fund proves otherwise.

Mr. Lynch only managed money for 12 years, turned prematurely gray, and retired early. His reported annual rate of return was 29 percent and his fund became the largest mutual fund in the business. His record does not subtract 3 percent to buy the fund and 3 percent annually to pay for the tax consequences. Nor does it reflect the capital gain taxes to sell the fund after he stopped managing money in 1990.

Mr. Lynch is a hero to some, including members of my own family. They say that those that can perform do and those that can't write, lecture, commentate, and advertise. He went on to help advertise his fund and write books about his investing style. But he didn't beat Berkshire. And Fidelity is still making money off his previous performance a decade later.

Mr. Lynch and Fidelity didn't make their money by picking stocks. Both of them made their personal fortunes by charging a fee to manage the fund. Almost immediately their return on money management was greater than the return on the Magellan fund. Investors would have been better off to own Fidelity if it were a publicly traded company than to own their funds.

Mr. Lynch outperformed in his first five years and underperformed in his last years. He actually lost money in his last year, something Berkshire has never done. Mr. Lynch is famed but is not a classic—and never will be.

John Templeton is also considered a money master but is not a classic. He too has made his money by charging a fee. Mr. Templeton has moved offshore to keep his fund management fees from government taxation.

As a side note, Mr. Templeton told an audience in Toronto in answer to my question regarding index funds, that too much money will flow into just 500 stocks ballooning the value thereby creating market under-performance. His theory hasn't been proven in the past 10 years. I think his advice was suspect because index funds don't have an entrance or exit fee, charge ⅐th the annual cost and are far more tax friendly compared to his funds.

Lynch, Templeton, Soros, Gabelli, and all the rest are not really money masters and haven't been proven over time. History will show that they made their money from the friction costs of other people's money. Unlike Buffett, they made their money by charging a fee, not by investing in the actual investments they recommended for others.

History has shown and will continue to record Berkshire's classic investment style of market out-performance, value, long term, deferred taxes, circle of competence, a small number of widely respected companies, wholly owned operating companies, no dividends, and ownership loyalty. Becoming a classic takes time. And time proves everything.

79 It's More Than What You Read

Reading the transcripts from the annual meeting weekend, Berkshire's press conference, and Charlie Munger's Wesco Financial [AMEX:WSE] annual meetings are great to add to your financial education. In fact you will read about some rather unique financial, investment and life concepts and ideas.

But the annual meeting weekend has become more than what you read. This is why attendance is so rewarding. It's what you hear. It's what you observe. It's whom you talk with. It's about what everyone wants to talk about. It's ideas that are shared. It's the networking. It's the discussion. It's the debates.

It's the continental breakfast with worldwide shareholders at the surrounding Omaha hotels. It's the local hospitality. It's what you won't read in any transcript or news story. Here are some non-transcript and non-reported observations. Berkshire is about who you meet, what you see and hear as much as what you read.

If you were fortunate to attend different shareholder related parties and receptions in Omaha over the weekend you would have witnessed a very accessible company chairman. Mr. Buffett and his family are available all weekend for photos, autographs, and handshakes. Berkshire is a family oriented company. If you wanted to meet and greet the chairman you have many opportunities.

The chairman is accessible, approachable and everywhere. Mr. Buffett attends as many shareholder related receptions that he can. On Friday before the meeting he attended no less than six receptions.

Mr. Buffett even makes himself available to the media with a press conference that is like a mini annual meeting. Democratically each member of the working media is able to ask questions in the order that they registered for the press conference. No question is edited or pre-screened. No question is dismissed as too elementary, stupid, or irrelevant. Thirty-five more questions in addition to the ones asked during the annual meeting.

Berkshire's shareholder group is the most literate and financially astute collection of people that you will meet. They read everything. They carry books.

Berkshire shareholders come to Omaha for their continuing financial, investment and life education without any need for a diploma, continuing educational credits, or resume credentials. This is a self-motivated, self-learning, and inquisitive group. This is a group defined by their love of learning and quest for knowledge and truth.

One shareholder brings his pre-teen daughters to expose them to the financial education and the financial truth in the parental hope that one day they may realize that their father gave them a foundation of financial learning from a master.

The operating mangers bring their spouses and family to the annual weekend. And everywhere you see Warren you will see his daughter and his sons. Sunday night at Warren's favorite steakhouse, Gorats, is a family affair with the whole Buffett family sitting down for a meal at the reserved head table.

Even the company video is a family affair. Daughter Susie produced the video and son Peter arranged the music, and Warren and his wife Susie sang the songs. This is one creative and musically talented family.

The video is a tribute to the extended Berkshire family and a tribute and appreciation of the operating managers and the 90,000 plus employees that make up this great company. Experiencing the company video is another reason to attend. It is difficult to describe.

Like a master politician, Berkshire's chairman is patient and calm with all questioners, autograph seekers, the media, and would be competitors. When an 'investor' suggests that his methods of tech stock selection resulted in record breaking results, Mr. Buffett suggested he distribute business cards to prospective clients.

Friend and foe on a democratic basis share microphones. First in line, first in question. Some even use their two minutes of fame to ask more than a question but to lecture, to profess, to promote, to suggest, to criticize, to commend, to toast, to philosophize, to politicize, to recommend, to request, and to brag. You name it.

Most of all the annual meeting weekend is unique in that it is an opportunity for investors to become educated about their investment in Berkshire, their management team, their operating subsidiaries, the marketable securities, the economy, investments other than Berkshire, commodities, real estate, foreign investments, politics, life, social security, taxation, partnerships, family, charity, estate planning, financial truth, momentum investing, the stock market, and the world, to name just a few.

You can take notes to increase your comprehension, read the transcripts afterward or merely sit and listen. Either way you will become a more educated investor. You walk away informed, amused, and wiser.

It is only by attending and networking do you realize how smart shareholders are drawn to Omaha. You begin to see first hand that you are mighty fine company when you strike up a conversation with fellow owners. These are your partners and you have self selected yourself to be part of this self-defined group.

Everyone is treated the same. No shareholders are given preferential treatment. Every shareholder is given the same information at the same time as any Wall Street analyst. There are no senior partners or junior partners. There is no class system that you may find in other publicly traded companies with institutional owners getting inside and earlier information.

The meeting is as democratic as it can he. Shareholders willing to stand in line get better seats. Box seats are not reserved for 'A' shareholders. And 'B' shareholders are not asked to sit in back. If you want to ask a question just get there early and sit by a microphone. Every shareholder is treated like a partner.

If you haven't attended in the past and haven't made it a priority, this is a strong recommendation to do so next year. You can read the transcripts and other people's accounts but Berkshire is more than what you read.

80 Misunderstood

Berkshire, like most things rarely found, is generally misunderstood. This is no surprise to the long-term shareholder. Legends are often misunderstood.

Recently, the press reported that Berkshire had captured 20 percent of the world's silver supply. Berkshire bought 130 million ounces of silver for $1 billion dollars.

Two ways the press misunderstood: one, a $1 billion investment for Berkshire is a non-event no matter what it is buying. Two, this investment is not a divergence for Berkshire. Value—whether it be in equities, bonds, preferred stock, a wholly owned business, or commodities like silver—is still value.

The real story is the extraordinary discipline Mr. Buffett demonstrates by first buying silver in the 1960's and then following the investment for over 30 years before purchasing 20 percent of the above ground supply. How many investment managers would closely follow anything for over 30 years before making a sizeable investment? In an investing world where the average hold is 13 months or less, I couldn't name one other investor or investment company with the wisdom to watch an investment for three decades before buying in. Instead, much of the media focus on the marketable securities, the purchases and sales, not the operating companies.

Even a recent book about Mr. Buffett redefined his investment style. This book helps readers misunderstand Berkshire by creating words such as toll bridge. It doesn't name in advance the three major acquisitions Berkshire made last year. But Berkshire is such a phenomenon that it is easy to understand such misinformation. Let me count the ways of misunderstanding:

(1) high price
(2) no dividends

(3) no stock splits
(4) long-term holdings
(5) executive compensation
(6) value
(7) tax management
(8) no earnings dilution
(9) concentration
(10) costs matter
(11) partnership attitude
(12) owner designated charities
(13) loyalty
(14) circle of competence
(15) owner discounts
(16) float
(17) bear market preparedness
(18) no tech stocks

One of the biggest misunderstandings is the so called "Buffett Premium". How can a stock consistently trade at a discount and be undervalued but be labeled a premium by the media?

Berkshire is misunderstood as a mutual fund or a conglomerate when it is better classified as an insurance company. Berkshire is often characterized as an assortment of non-related business enterprises. It fits Berkshire but doesn't fit the model of the financial press.

The fact that Berkshire is not invited to join the S&P 500 Index is a great example of it being misunderstood. A U.S. based company acquiring another S&P 500 company with a combined market cap of over $100 billion is not included in an index that supposedly represents the 500 largest companies. The reason: too thinly traded and a lack of liquidity with only a few hundred shares traded daily. As long as Berkshire continues to be ignored by financial analysts and financial educators, intelligent debate won't happen.

You're talking one great investment when you combine (#52) Unknown with (#80) Misunderstood. For a current shareholder or even as a perspective owner, misunderstanding by the media, the competition, and the investor population at large is a good thing. To be misunderstood is to be ignored and unwanted. This creates a great opportunity for shareholders that will last.

81 Value Investing

B erkshire has redefined the term value investing. Mr. Buffett considers the two terms to be redundant. If investing weren't the pursuit of finding an investment at a good value then what is it? Investing is the commitment of money in order to gain a profit. In order to gain a profit you must see value immediately, soon or sometime in the future. Investing is the realization of value.

Berkshire continues to redefine value. Some have tried to separate investing styles into growth and value, but Berkshire considers both to be interrelated. Growth is always a part of value.

Value is sometimes mistaken as bottom feeding or bargain hunting or, in Mr. Buffett's words, "cigar butt investing." Cigar butt investing is to look for neglected investments that have a few free earnings puffs left in them. This method considers the short-term profit over the long-term business decline, poor performance, or even bankruptcy. Berkshire is named after a cigar butt investment: Berkshire Hathaway textile mills. Mr. Buffett has admitted to more than a few cigar butt investments in his career. I could probably personally open a cigar butt factory with my former investments.

Value investing is not to be confused with mediocrity. Coke and Gillette were and still are great business franchises available at a good value. Value not only includes the component of price but also involves the management of the business. A great business with bad management is not a good investment value. A mediocre business with superior management doesn't deliver value either.

Most believe value stocks to have high dividend yields, a low price to earnings ratio, and a low price to book value. Once again Berkshire presents us with an irony—a value stock with no dividend.

Most day traders do not consider the concept of value with their investing mania. Traders in general aren't concerned with the gradual realization of long-term value but rather the belief that they can sell a stock for a price greater than they paid for it within six months or less. Short-term price movements are usually a function of supply and demand combined with emotion. Long-term price is a function of the underlying business value. Great value is rarely achieved in the short run.

Berkshire teaches us about intrinsic value. Simply stated: how much cash should be invested to get cash in return over time or what someone would pay for such a stream of cash? Mr. Buffett defines intrinsic value as 'a hard to calculate but crucial measure of business value equal to the discounted present value of the cash that can be taken out of a business during its remaining life'.

If Berkshire stands for anything, it stands for value. Where else do you learn about cigar butt investing, taxes, costs, present value of a stream of payments, management, business valuation, ten-year measurement, growth and value?

82 Very Rare Talent

Superior investment management is a very rare talent. Tens of thousands offer their money management services and millions more do it on their own with less than mediocre results.

Berkshire has performed this service in an extraordinary fashion and like a great athlete, has made it look easy.

It's ironic that people who charge a money management fee generally do not add value and even those who attempt this necessary service on their own pay an even bigger cost. The obvious costs are the management fees if you use a money manager or mutual fund, plus transaction fees and taxes. The less obvious cost and the biggest cost is the difference in your net annual returns compared to the overall market and Berkshire.

Furthermore, you don't get what you pay for with the typical investment manager. You would think that the more you pay the more you get or you get what you pay for. This isn't so. You pay less at Berkshire and get a lot more added value.

Fidelity, the largest mutual fund group, would charge $1 billion to manage Berkshire compared to Berkshire's modest management fee of $6 million; a billion more to perform less.

Buffett watchers seem to fall into two camps: those who admire and those who want to be like him. Admirers, like myself, don't spend much time trying to figure out how Berkshire performs. We want to know why we should invest, not how Berkshire performs its investment magic. This group just knows and trusts their investments in the hands of proven professionals.

Long-term owners have no choice but to admire. Having added two zeros to their Berkshire holdings over the past 20 years, the tax consequence of selling and competing would be too great. Admirers, possibly from experience, know how difficult the investment management job is of truly adding value.

This first group of admirers is open to everyone. The second group is open to a few.

The first group is the sports fan. The second group is the highly paid athlete or weekend warrior.

The second group of Buffett watchers wants to know how. They are the Warren Wannabes. They monitor his every move, pick apart his weaknesses, second guess his moves, and strongly believe that they can do better. This group believes that investment management is easy and beating the average of all the rest is within reach. This group tends to be young, inexperienced and or extremely well compensated. Most believe momentum and technology stocks are the way to beat Berkshire.

Money management is like golf. Millions play. Most are average at best. Thousands can shoot par. Just a handful can consistently shoot under par.

In the United States alone, over 100 million people need to manage their money. Most are not very good at it. Tens of thousands offer investment management services for a steep fee and only a very few have this rare talent of adding value.

Unlike golf, the average investor can guarantee par by purchasing an index fund but less than 10 percent make this wise choice. That means 90 percent of all investors believe they can beat the collective wisdom of the market. This is a mathematical impossibility.

Unlike golf, the average investor doesn't even know what is par. When he or she hires a professional, the professional doesn't measure against par.

Mutual funds like to look better by measuring against their average peer fund instead of their respective index. Unlike golf, age, wisdom, and experience count. In fact, the senior tour is the preferred choice. Unlike golf, retirement isn't mandatory. If you can find a good pro you don't want him or her to retire. Unlike golf, the average investor and 'professional' is two percentage points over par. Five percentage points over par if you include the tax costs. Unlike golf, the collective wisdom and talent of a group, like an investment club, will not add value.

There's no other business quite like the money management business. It's the only business that I know that just about everyone thinks they are good at it, but facts prove otherwise. It's the only business I know that you can charge more for providing less. The barriers to entry are low so many enter this field believing they will add value. Once they find out that only a very, very few have talent, it's too late to get out.

The investment business looks easy, so many investors do it themselves. To millions more it looks complicated, so they hire 'professionals'. The lucky few, who know how very, very rare money management talent is, hired Berkshire.

The best owners of Berkshire, besides long-term owners, are investors who have done everything else. Investors who know how difficult the job is, yet how easy it appears.

83 Inefficient Market Theory

Berkshire represents the opposite of the efficient market theorists. The efficient market theory states that whatever is known about a stock is quickly built into the price of the stock. There will be some divergence between the stock price and the stock news both rumored and true. But sooner, not later, the stock price is accurately portrayed.

The efficient market theory is taught in the best business schools and is practiced by institutional and private index investors. This theory makes most followers give up on valuation exercises because the market knows best. Why try to beat the general consensus of the market.

Berkshire proves this theory wrong in two ways. To determine value, Berkshire has consistently looked at the present value of a stock. Mr. Buffett has publicly proven that business valuation is an art more than a science. If business valuation were easy, every financial analyst and stock rating service would be wealthy.

Second, Berkshire's own stock is an example of the inefficient market theory. If the market took everything that is known about Berkshire, the stock would be priced closer to its true value instead of consistently being undervalued.

Efficient market theorists would want to know more not less about Berkshire. More analysts would cover the stock. Instead, just a few analysts report on Berkshire. For Berkshire owners, it is probably best that the efficient market theory is such a widely held belief.

The secret to success in this business is weak competition. If Berkshire's competition generally believes in the opposite theory and doesn't even try, this will create opportunities .

It's sad to think that our business school students are starting their careers with such a handicap. But I am optimistic that one day the time-tested Berkshire theories will replace long held academic dogma and be required reading by finance students and practitioners. Time has a way of testing theories, and eventually truth prevails.

84 Turn Off the Noise

Make Berkshire your largest holding and turn off the noise. There is no need to read the financial section of your local newspaper and no need to watch financial programs on TV. End your subscriptions to financial rating services. Stop reading newsletters about the market. Turn off the noise.

The financial press is bought and paid for by financial products and services. If there wasn't any financial media, there would be no method to advertise financial doctors, get rich quick schemes, financial supermarkets, money cure-alls, super human money managers, tax favored products—any and all things that you don't need.

My two best investment lessons—indexing and Berkshire— did not come out of financial media noise. But make no mistake, the financial industry needs the media. Objective reporting is rare. Have you ever read a story saying the whole mutual fund industry has not added value? You probably never will.

Financial reporting is about emotion: The extremes between greed and fear, investing with your heart. The world of financial media is about urgency, breaking news, and self-important 'investment professionals'. Many of these 'professionals' talk about stocks they own, so viewers, listeners, and or readers go out and buy the stock and drive the price up or they talk about stocks they have shorted so the public drives the price down. When money managers participate in the media they make money. They create awareness of their products and services and generate interest in their financial transactions.

There is so much bad information, and so many investment alternatives that the average investor can be overwhelmed. In the investment information age we are swimming with lots of bad information in shark infested waters.

The media operates under the same old dogma taught in schools. They often sponsor investing programs targeted to schools and the general population. These simulated trading contests teach among other bad stuff, short term trading. They lure the uneducated, the young, the unsuspecting to believe that money can be quickly made with advancements in technology.

The media doesn't teach and inform about the long-term philosophies of Berkshire Hathaway. Have you ever heard the media say that money managers are a rare breed? Even the ranking services and the general financial press, rank mediocre results against a peer group instead of a true index. The media suggest more products and services instead of educating about the current choices. When have you seen the media recall a guest commentator and play back advice given some time in the past and ask for accountability, measurement, and comparison?

Financial noise creates stars. The louder and more extreme the better. Extreme is interesting and entertaining. Volatility sells. Investors want to believe in gurus. In reality, noise doesn't help you. It just confuses you. Noise does not educate. Too much noise leads to indecision.

Generally, Mr. Buffett will not do interviews. Recently, he did a sweeps period interview on a network (ABC), of which Berkshire owns a sizeable percentage. This important information was declared at the beginning of the interview. Berkshire will not participate in the noise even though it has other significant media ownership. Mr. Buffett has never and will never talk about stocks it is acquiring or thinking about owning. Mr. Buffett will never recommend the purchase of Berkshire, even though he has 99 percent of his net worth in Berkshire.

Do yourself a favor and turn off the financial noise and turn on the writings and wisdom of Mr. Buffett. His chairman's letters are available free at www.berkshirehathaway.com/.

85 Capital Allocation

Berkshire is the best capital allocator in the business. Most businesses excel at doing what they are good at and then reach a point of excess capital. This can be an opportunity or a problem.

The challenge at any successful enterprise is to properly deploy its excess capital. Management can acquire a competitor, diversify outside its area of strength, and or return the capital in the form of dividends to its owners. The handicap of dividends is that corporations are taxed twice, once at the corporate level and again at the ownership level.

Capital allocation is probably one of the biggest weaknesses of the average business. It is difficult to manage a business and properly evaluate other businesses for investment. Often, a business has met its downfall by diversifying outside its core business. How many times have you read about 'one time charges' due to poor acquisitions or expansions? Just because you are successful at one specific business doesn't automatically make you good at valuing, acquiring, and managing other businesses. In fact being very successful at one business will statistically make you unlikely to succeed at most others.

Berkshire has made a name for itself with its expertise in business valuation. Few have the ability to take excess capital and deploy it with such remarkable skill. The chief strategy of Berkshire's management is to take excess capital from its operating businesses and find the optimal home for it.

Individuals are faced with the same challenge as every successful enterprise. Individuals have capital in the form of wages, dividends, interest, capital gains, business sales, gifts, estates, inheritances, retirement programs and savings that need to be allocated. Each of us allocates our capital every day. Some are good at it, others bad.

Individuals can fall prey to thinking that because they have excess capital to invest they must be good at allocation, evaluation, acquisition, and management. They aren't. What they are good at is quick disposal. Mr. Buffett has said that he would rather have cash burning a hole in Berkshire's pocket, than resting comfortably in someone else's.

Individual investors spend 92 percent of their time on stock/fund selection and market timing. Research has shown us that investment return is just the opposite of most investor's behavior. An investment's return is four percent market timing, four percent stock/fund selection, and 92 percent asset allocation.

Isn't it ironic that we spend our time in areas of little consequence to our overall return; the area that is most important to contributing positive results is greatly ignored. Just eight percent of the average investor's time is spent on asset allocation.

Day traders are a good example of this time allocation irony. Most if not all of their time is spent on stock/fund selection, acquisition, disposal, and timing the market. Little time is spent on capital allocation.

Look at the Internet investment bulletin boards, including the Motley Fool, the site I chose to write this series. All the time and energy is spent on market evaluation, timing, and stock selection, but very little to capital allocation.

Asset allocation is determining what percentage of the portfolio should be in the different asset classes: equities, bonds, commodities, real estate and cash—and when to change the percentages in each asset class. It's also about how much to change. Interest rates and overall corporate earnings need to be considered.

Berkshire has stressed repeatedly that its first choice use of capital is to acquire wholly owned businesses. If Mr. Buffet likes a business, he wants to own all of it, not part of it. In the future Berkshire's capital allocation will be buying entire companies, like GenRe, Dairy Queen, Executive Jet, Flight Safety, and GEICO. Capital allocation is usually a long-term decision, which is why it gets little attention.

So we are quick to blame businesses for weak capital allocation. But individual investors are just as weak in this area. Why not let the world's best capital allocator do this important job for you? You know he will do a good job because he is doing it for himself at the same time.

A decision to own Berkshire is a decision to allocate your capital where it is treated the best. To make your own capital allocation decisions is to compete against the brightest and most skillful.

86 Intelligent Investing

B erkshire eliminates the emotion from investing. It invests with logic and intellect. As a business owner, I can tell you that on any given day the price of my business varies from real cheap to priceless. Depending on the day and the challenges, most businesses are subject to emotional valuation. When the problems are great, the business value is low. Conversely, when things are humming along, the value rises. Fortunately for most small business owners a market environment doesn't exist to quickly dispose of a business.

Investors are no different. When things are going up they don't want to sell. When their investment declines they can't wait for it to recover its cost basis so they can sell it. Most will wait without a logic test and wait and wait before selling. It hurts too much to realize a loss. Besides, it isn't officially a loss until it's sold. The majority of investors, both individual and institutional, are emotional investors. They feel good when the portfolio goes up and terrible when it goes down.

- Intelligent investing means never having to sell. If the price of your few chosen securities goes down, you buy more or simply wait for the long-term realization of its underlying value.
- Emotional investing means revolving ownership chairs. The average NASDAQ stock is held just six months. One stock was recently traded so frequently that its complete ownership changed eight times in one day.
- Intelligent investing waits for the best opportunities. This style knows that many opportunities are ahead and the longer it waits the better.
- Emotional investing jumps quickly, frequently, and time is always of the essence.
- Intelligent investing believes that you only need a few good ideas for an investment lifetime.
- Emotional investing believes you never lose money taking a profit.
- Intelligent investing takes the emotion out and will often dollar cost average and or buy an index fund.
- Emotional investing takes the intelligence out and will leverage its short term bets.
- Intelligent investing will hold forever. To death do they part.
- Emotional investing will sell within minutes if the price is right.
- Intelligent investing will buy in a concentrated fashion.

- Emotional investing will never put all its eggs in one basket but would broadly diversify out of ignorance.
- Intelligent investing allows you to turn off the market.
- Emotional investing forces you to watch the ticker tape and tune in all the noise.
- Intelligent investing considers the tax consequences.
- Emotional investing generally disregards taxes as just something to worry about in the future. Besides, if you're making money it's just a cost of doing business. If you have some losses you can use them to offset some gains.
- Intelligent investing considers the overall rate of return net of taxes and costs. And compares this net return to a benchmark.
- Emotional investing is about an overall feeling you get about an investment and your style.
- Intelligent investing permits the hiring of more intelligent minds to perform the investment duties.
- Emotional investors believe that they know best.
- Intelligent investing is about capital allocation.
- Emotional investing is about market timing and stock selection.
- Intelligent investing is boring.
- Emotional investing is exciting. It's about technology. It's about momentum. It's this new thing.
- Intelligent investing is about inactivity.
- Emotional investing is about rapid-fire, constant trading, and replacing those in favor yesterday with those in favor today.
- Intelligent investing is about self-reliance.
- Emotional investing is about relying on a broker or financial advisor. They take credit for the ups and have someone to blame when things go down.
- Intelligent investing is about loyalty.
- Emotional investing is about what have you done for me this week.
- Intelligent investing is using your brain.

- Emotional investing is using your heart and feelings.
- Intelligent investing is that practiced by Mr. Buffett and Berkshire Hathaway.
- Emotional investing is Mr. Market, taught by Mr. Buffett's teacher, Ben Graham. Mr. Market is a manic depressive, subject to wide swings in emotion. Intelligent investors wait for the natural occurrence and then jump on opportunities. Emotional investors burn out.

87 Peaceful Night's Sleep

Berkshire is an investment for those who enjoy their sleep. If you own Berkshire you don't need to check the stock price or wake up in the middle of the night to see what the Asian markets have done. Traders who have a difficult time sleeping generally have too much risk, don't understand the risks they have assumed, or are ignorant to the risks associated with their trading.

If you're not sleeping then you have too much risk or lack important investment information.

Berkshire is not about price. Berkshire is not about markets. Berkshire is about value.

Although risk and volatility are not necessarily related, Berkshire has 20 percent less volatility than the overall market.

Berkshire's beta is .80 with the market at 1.00. It probably shouldn't surprise you that the beta of technology and momentum stocks ranges from 1.25 to 3.00. You can lose a lot of sleep with a high beta stock.

As long as you have purchased Berkshire at or below its intrinsic value (IV) you'll get plenty of sleep. Since Berkshire always trades below IV you can own Berkshire anytime and anywhere.

Those who have bought Berkshire only to monitor its price movement don't understand why they purchased the stock. Those who sell Berkshire soon after purchasing it don't understand why they bought either.

Even stock arbitrators who buy and sell A and B shares to take advantage of the 1A = 30B ratio don't have the big picture. Why spend time, transaction costs, and tax costs getting an extra 1 or 2 percent when the overall stock is up 33 percent annually.

Because it is so thinly traded, less than 500 A shares trade daily, the price movement is usually directly associated with supply and demand. If the stock price moves down then more people are selling than buying. The opposite is true as well. Since little is known about earnings and earnings are subject to big swings, the price may adjust with quarterly earnings announcements, annual report releases, acquisition notices, and the annual meetings. Over time the price of the stock will eventually meet its intrinsic value and generally grow at the same rate as the underlying book value (approximately 25 percent annually). Occasionally the stock price may get ahead of itself, but generally the market price trades below its intrinsic value.

Owners of Berkshire can sleep at night knowing that the price has never failed to achieve its previous high and bear markets will create more opportunities for Berkshire than any other enterprise. A great leader and loyal owners are great sleep aids.

If you read and agree with the owner's manual, this investment is right for you. If you purchased the stock or it was given to you and you don't agree with the principles highlighted in the owner's manual, then sell the stock.

Even if you have been unfortunate enough to have purchased Berkshire 20 percent too high, you can still sleep at night knowing the intrinsic value will meet and exceed its historically high price within a year.

88 Independent Thought

Thinking for yourself, independent of what others think or say is a very important investment concept.

Most of us are looking for validation of our beliefs, philosophies, and principles particularly when it comes to our money and our investments.

If you're like me the first thing you look at in the stock pages are the Dow averages and/or the most actively traded issues (the volume leaders). This is what everyone else is doing. This is a summary of groupthink.

The collective summary of how you, everyone else, and I think and act in the stock market is the market. The only way to beat the market over time is to have independent thought.

It takes a lot of willpower, courage, strength, energy, power, and confidence to move against the crowd.

Most of us (fortunately not all of us) are wired to concern ourselves with others. We have learned to survive by forming communities, laws and rules of behavior. We patronize restaurants that have been voted the best by local readers or restaurant critics.

We concern ourselves with critical reviews and top grossing movies. We read books because they are best sellers. We are a society caught up with ratings, stars, rankings, and rave reviews.

Why should our investments be any different?

Investors want to be ahead of change. Ahead of everyone else. We want our stocks in the news, heralded by the media, talked about on Wall Street Week, on the cover of Forbes, going from a few dollars to a zillion overnight.

We are taught to think and act like the collective—which is the opposite of what successful investors need to be.

Look at institutions, mutual funds, margin traders and even the so-called gurus. Everyone wants to please the crowd, do what other people are doing and follow "groupthink."

Groupthinkers concern themselves with market analysis. Independent thinkers concern themselves with business analysis.

My best idea didn't come from following collective thought or groupthink. Instead I asked who is the best at investing and is he available to manage my money?

How much does he charge? What are his investment principles and do I agree with them? What can I read about him? Is his performance of public record and audited? How has he been able to outperform groupthink (the market)?

The best owners use groupthink to compare how their independently thought investments have done over time.

Berkshire is the ultimate investment of independent thought.

It doesn't matter what PaineWebber or First Boston thinks about Berkshire. It doesn't matter that the marketplace has high regard for our chairman and little regard for Berkshire's stock.

It doesn't matter that groupthink believes Berkshire is about one man and when that one man 'retires' the stock will be worthless.

It doesn't matter that groupthink rallies a short-term knowledge of a stock Berkshire is rumored or even known to have purchased yet undervalues the parent company's stock even though it just finished buying the very same hot stock.

All in all Berkshire is better off if it has a group of shareholders that arrived by independent thought.

89 World's Largest Foundation

Berkshire is the vehicle for Mr. Buffett to create the world's largest foundation: $30 billion and growing at a rate of 31 percent a year.

To own Berkshire is to participate in this incredible act of public service. Each individual Class A shareholder gets to participate in the owner designated charity program each year. With their Berkshire stock they can one day fund their own philanthropic program.

Mr. Buffett makes each of us think about our service to others. In fact, Berkshire represents all that is good about capitalism: To make money by fulfilling the needs and wants of others, then taking those profits and passing them on to the world at large through a foundation. Remember, the foundation will one day belong to the world.

Mr. Buffett has recently stated that he plans to fund six different areas that the world's governments are not funding. Pressed for an example on a recent interview, he stated that he thought trying to curtail nuclear information was an important world need.

He isn't sure how to cure the problems, but he knows they will need money. Solutions are outside his area of competence. Funding the solution makers is well within his expertise.

Mr. Buffett makes each class A owner think about the community where the owner lives and what to do with the abundant wealth Berkshire has and will continue to create.

Actually creating the world's largest foundation is the natural outgrowth of any successful investment model. Long-term concentrated holdings with minimum friction costs in the form of transactions and taxes. The more successful the investment program is the greater the size of the foundation. Foundation size is the ultimate measurement of an investor's skill. Foundation meaningfulness is ultimately the measurement of the investor's wisdom and compassion.

Some would argue that Mr. Buffett should begin to distribute his vast fortune now and not wait for the passing of himself and his wife. But once again he shows us to stick with what you know best. He doesn't know the answers to our world problems. He does know that the problems need money to be solved. By sticking to what he is good at, making money and creating wealth, he can play a very important role in making the world a better place.

There's something fun and meaningful about being part of a bigger mission. Somehow it feels better to build wealth for making the world a better place than to just think about the enjoyment of wealth for yourself and your family.

Berkshire is better when shared. I hope some of the Buffett Foundation goes to help the world's financial educational programs teach young people the Berkshire investment model.

90 Active Mind

Berkshire's chairman has always had an active mind. Mr. Buffett keeps his mind sharp by reading daily and playing bridge. His body may grow old but his mind will always be ten years ahead of most.

Someone with an active mind stays forever young. He or she reads and demonstrates him or herself through wit, wisdom, and writings. There's a direct relationship between superior intellect and wit. And anyone who has attended any of the annual meetings knows the incredible quick wit of the chairman.

Those who think Mr. Buffett doesn't understand technology may not know he plays bridge on the Internet to exercise his active mind. Some 10 to 15 hours per week you can find him at www.okbridge.com under the code name 'tbone' representing his favorite food. Mr. Buffett has promised that if the markets show greater value he will cut back on his bridge playing to make more acquisitions.

Mr. Buffett has played bridge since childhood and plays with other active people like Katharine Graham, from *The Washington Post* and Bill Gates, founder of Microsoft. Mr. Buffett has become a better player by playing bridge online. He has done well enough to get in the final round of a live online bridge world class tournament. That's pretty good for someone who supposedly doesn't understand technology.

Bridge and investment success have several things in common. One, you need to use your intellect. Two, a smarter player can beat someone with lucky cards. Three, wisdom, experience, and applied intelligence matter. Four, the better players are generally older and more experienced. Five, as you get information you need to modify your behavior. Six, it pays to have a good partner. Last and most important, you need to act in a way that is best for your partner.

Berkshire always acts in the best interest of its partners. Remember number one of the owner's principles is Berkshire's partnership attitude.

Although some mistake the stock market as a game, Berkshire doesn't 'play' the market. It buys businesses at a good value and until death do they part.

An active mind betters the odds of having a long life, but certainly doesn't guarantee it and fortunately for me, you don't need to be a genius to be good at investing. Having an active mind helps but it's not a requirement. A great intellect without character is of little use.

The smartest investors recognize the difficulty of winning at investments so they either buy an index fund to match the market and beat 90 percent of everything else. Or, they hire smarter minds to do the investing for them.

An active mind like Mr. Buffett's never stops. Fortunately for shareholders, the chairman's intellect is always working for them.

91 Always Good Surprises

With Berkshire there are never bad surprises. All surprises are good. Each day serious investors scan the financial pages to uncover what they don't know but need to know about their investments. Surprises are the downfall of many investments.

Seasoned investors concern themselves with research reports, charts, comparisons, earnings, analysts' recommendations, and among other things, whisper numbers. First, the analysts project the next quarter's earnings, and based on a consensus, an earning's expectation is set. As earning's announcement dates draw near a new 'whisper number' (a new number below, at, or above the earlier estimate) surfaces.

The price of a stock will either rise or fall depending on how close actual earnings meet or exceed whispered earnings. Sometimes a company will preannounce its earnings to get the projected, whispered and actual earnings in line. This exercise is all short-term and transaction-oriented.

Berkshire doesn't have a stock whisperer. Whisper numbers run contrary to Berkshire's beliefs and owner's principles. Since few analysts follow Berkshire, there are no 'professional' earnings projections, whisper numbers, earnings disappointments, a need to preannounce, or any negative surprises. All Berkshire news is good.

Even a surprise like a $1 billion super catastrophe insurance claim, possibly a California earthquake, will only impact Berkshire at less than one percent of its financial holdings.

Everyday we hear about companies needing to take a one-time charge for management miscalculations or for acquisitions gone wrong. How many times have you been surprised when you hear about lawsuits, rapid technology changes, obsolescence, competition, government interventions, world economic changes, Federal Reserve announcements, widespread sell offs, management resignations, employee slow downs or strikes, need for capital infusion, crooked management, greenmail, bankruptcy, corporate raiders, unfriendly takeovers, massive layoffs, sector rotation, commodity scarcity, and exorbitant management compensation packages? Under Murphy's Law everything that can go wrong with an investment portfolio will. It's the surprises you don't know about that can hurt your financial well being.

Berkshire manages its surprises by using every opportunity to lower investor expectations. Wise companies restrict media attention and exposure to keep surprises positive. Even with large media ownership, Berkshire executives don't do interviews and don't release marketable security purchases until 13 months later.

Companies love to hear that Berkshire is buying its stock. That means the stock is attractive, stable and management and employees will get no outside involvement. Berkshire doesn't buy to make changes. It values a company more if it's not subject to surprises.

With investments you need to manage surprises. Surprises are generally bad. The price of a stock always goes down faster than it goes up and a stock's slow climb can lose all of its gains in a matter of minutes when surprises are announced.

At Berkshire, no change is good. No news is good. Little analyst coverage is good. Surprises are always good.

92 For Owners Only

Berkshire is for owners only not traders. There's a big difference.

- Owners are long term (five years or greater).
- Traders are short term (less than 13 months).
- Owners are a very small group.
- Traders represent most of Wall Street, individual investors, money managers, and mutual funds.
- Owners look past the latest quarterly earnings.
- Traders run after the latest earnings announcement.
- Owners desire stability and predictability.
- Traders want change.

- Owners know that 75 percent of the time the market rises and a rising tide lifts all boats.
- Traders are happy with a 5 to 10 percent short-term gain and are always annualizing their gains.
- Owners are concerned about transaction costs.
- Traders view friction costs (transaction and taxes) as a cost of doing business.
- Owners concern themselves with the tax consequences.
- Traders see the government sharing in the capital gains and losses equally.
- Owners don't have capital losses.
- Traders think capital losses are a cost of business.
- Owners build with brick and concrete, reinforce to prevent weather destruction, and use a moat for safety.
- Traders rent temporary housing, and frequently move.
- Owners are pillars in the community.
- Traders are gypsies.
- Owners invest in their own homes and communities.
- Traders are hobos and build other people's communities.
- Owners build main street.
- Traders build Wall Street.
- Owners own the casino.
- Traders gamble at the casino.
- Owners' language is one of belonging.
- Traders' language is one of transaction and action verbs; buy, sell, accumulate, attractive, hold, trade, going forward, upgrade, downgrade, watch, etc.
- Owners concentrate their holdings and are very knowledgeable.
- Traders diversify out of ignorance.
- Owners take possession of their stock certificates.
- Traders leave certificates in the hands of their brokers, ready to trade at a moment's notice.
- Owners are rational.
- Traders are emotional.
- Owners are concerned about the underlying value of the company.
- Traders focus on price.

- Owners look at the big picture.
- Traders view the short picture.
- Owners are loyal.
- Traders are traitors.
- Owners buy and use the company's products.
- Traders buy based on habit, price, and convenience with little regard for ownership and loyalty.
- Owners support management.
- Traders support whoever can affect the stock price.
- Owners like share repurchases.
- Traders like dividends.
- Owners support capital reinvestment to build for the future.
- Traders support anything that will temporarily move the stock price up.
- Owners think that the way to wealth is through long term ownership of an equity.
- Traders believe wealth is created by rapid-fire transactions.
- Owners have resources they want to protect and grow.
- Traders want more resources and are willing to risk more to get more.
- Ownership reduces risk.
- Trading increases risk.
- Owners want management to own a substantial share of the business.
- Traders want management to get stock options designed to benefit only if the stock price goes up.
- Owners plan to stay as long as the most loyal employee.
- Traders don't last as long as the most recent temporary mail clerk.
- Owners demand accurate accounting and everything straight and up on the balance sheet and income statement.
- Traders don't mind major items like management compensation left off the balance sheet and income statement. Leave it for the one-time big bath restructuring charge.
- Owners don't listen to brokers, gurus, pundits, financial publications, trading models, seminars, advisors, financial television programs or any of the rest.

- Traders listen to all the noise.
- Owners keep it simple.
- Traders make it complex.
- Owners are informed.
- Traders are misinformed.
- Owners win long term.
- Traders win short term.
- Owners own.
- Traders temporarily rent stock.
- Owners never retire.
- Traders burn out.
- Owners love traders. They eventually create market extremes. Traders are weak competitors. They try to buy low and sell high or buy high and sell higher, but sometimes they buy high and sell low.
- All owners will eventually get a good price because they have time on their side.

Ownership or trading is a choice. I believe most traders really want to be owners. In my case it took 30 years of being a trader to become an owner. I hope it doesn't take you as long. Remember, there's a reason why this book is titled *101 Reasons to Own the World's Greatest Investment*.

93 Creative Tax-free Dividends

Berkshire doesn't pay a traditional dividend; however, it is a big proponent of share repurchases. Share buybacks are a creative tax-free dividend.

Part of the Berkshire investment model is to buy a few widely respected companies, like Coke and Gillette, and sit on their board of directors. From the inside, Mr. Buffett suggests how these companies should allocate their excess earnings.

If they can't meet the simple test of investing their earnings to grow their business, Mr. Buffett suggests they pay shareholders a creative tax-free dividend or in other words, take the cash and buyback its own shares. This lowers the number of outstanding shares and raises the percentage ownership of each shareholder, and quickly returns value when the stock price is way undervalued.

When a company pays a dividend, it isn't allowed to deduct dividend payments as a business expense and when an owner receives a dividend he or she is taxed at the income rate, not the more favorable capital gains rate. The income tax rate may average 30 percent or higher and needs to be paid annually. The capital gain rate may average 20 percent and doesn't need to be paid unless there is a sale.

Coca Cola paid 56¢ per share in dividends in 1997 costing the company $1.4 billion representing 33.6 percent of its earnings. With a corporate tax rate of 31.8 percent this dividend cost Coke $441 million in non-deductible expenses and cost the individual shareholders (assuming 30 percent income tax rate) an additional $416 million. So the nearly $1.4 billion in dividends only nets a little more than $500 million in economic benefit to the owners.

Now let's look at the net economic benefit of Coca Cola's share repurchases. In 1997 Coke bought back $1.3 billion of its common stock. This took 10 million shares off the market and increased the owners share of the company by .4 percent, all without creating a taxable event. This is a creative tax-free dividend.

Coke's management should be congratulated for doing what is in the best interest of adding shareholder value. Over the past 13 years, Coke has bought back more than one billion of its shares. This represents 31 percent of the shares outstanding repurchased at an average price of $11.27.

Share repurchases are best when the stock is trading below its intrinsic value. Allocation of capital is a tricky business and Coke, Gillette, Washington Post, and Berkshire should feel that they have on their board the best value mind in the business.

Berkshire allocates earnings of its operating business to maximize creative tax-free dividends. With its acquisition of GenRe, Berkshire saved $45 million in a fourth quarter dividend payment by closing one day before the ex-dividend date. This is $45 million Berkshire doesn't need to pay out, $45 million Berkshire can now reallocate with the shareholders better net interest in mind, and this is $45 million that owners do not have to pay regular income taxes on.

Just in GenRe dividends, Berkshire will save shareholders $180 million annually in corporate non-deductible expenses and owners $180 million in taxable dividends. Dividends represented 18 percent of GenRe's earnings, which will now be in the hands of the world's greatest capital allocator.

Share repurchases need to be compared to the average stock market investor's psyche. Share buyback programs are double tax efficient and a long-term value. With an average hold of six months, the average NASDAQ stock market participant couldn't care less about share buyback programs.

If your motivation is price, then taxable dividends can pay you while you impatiently wait. If your investment motivation is value, than share buyback programs give you better economic benefit.

Remember your broker, financial advisor, money manager, and others in the financial industry make money on the friction costs of your transactions and are therefore not excited about share repurchases.

Even substantial billion-dollar mutual funds don't sit on the board of directors of the companies it owns for you. They are not compensated by how tax efficient their underlying companies are. They couldn't care about the impact of share repurchases because they are not long-term owners. By definition, with such a sizeable amount of the company owned by management, you never need to worry about your financial well-being. Berkshire is always looking out for its owners.

Remember this April 15 that your broker, financial advisor, money manager, and mutual fund have all sent you a tax bill. Berkshire has never sent a tax bill to its shareholders and probably never will.

94 Perpetual Gift

One of the most profound reasons to own Berkshire is the fact that it's a perpetual gift. It's the gift that keeps on giving. Besides the monetary rewards and gifts, the non-monetary paybacks from Berkshire are numerous—the philosophies, the beliefs, the principles, the life-style, the long-term orientation, value, results, admiration, and loyalty.

A good friend and fellow shareholder calls Berkshire the 'fine china'. On special occasions, you get it out to share with family and special friends. And when you do share it, you find the Berkshire message keeps coming back.

A spiritual investment enlightenment is how some may describe the Berkshire beacon. And when the light clicks on it has changed your life forever. In a recent *Forbes* magazine article, one long-term shareholder said, "There are three things in my life: God, Warren Buffett, and my wife and I'm not sure about the order of the first two."

In a religious fever you feel compelled to share your gift. You tell all who will listen—your family, friends, neighbors, club members, soccer moms, clients, suppliers, restaurant employees, and even the person sitting next to you on an airplane. The ones who get it tell their family and friends and so on. Eventually all gifts, like the circle of life, come back.

I shared Berkshire with a friend who has now taught me more about this investment than I would have discovered on my own. It's probably why the annual meeting is so important; the networking, the fellowship, the discovery.

At the last annual meeting, I met a doctor and his wife at the Omaha 114th Street Dairy Queen. They drove from Alabama for the weekend. He discovered Berkshire much like I did after mismanaging his investments. He spent quite a bit of time on the Internet talking about and defending Berkshire. Only a few listened to the doctor's gift.

New Berkshire shareholders are drawn to the Internet to discuss their financial enlightenment and gift because sometimes their spouses, friends, neighbors, parents, children, and grandchildren just don't get it.

Since few in the financial community will recommend Berkshire you stand alone in your beliefs until you find a fellow shareholder. The Internet is probably the fastest way to find someone who thinks alike.

In life you get what you give. Give loyalty, get loyalty. Give Berkshire, get Berkshire.

As for me, writing this book is a way of giving back. To understand something you need to teach or, in my case, write. It's been amazing to discover how much I actually know about Berkshire, and even more amazing to find out what I don't know. To serve, to contribute, to teach, to write, and to give are all reciprocal and perpetual.

Writing about Berkshire has also helped me cope with all the time I now have that I used to spend working on the investment process. Time: another gift from Berkshire that keeps on giving—time that I now can give my family, career, avocations, writings, community, and even local investment clubs.

95 No Gimmicks

There's no gimmick to Berkshire. You won't find derivatives, margin, options, unit investment trusts, shorting foreign currencies, hedge funds, offshore tricks, greenmail, hostile takeovers, or lawsuits.

You won't hear about Berkshire on any infomercial boasting get rich quick schemes. You'll never hear Mr. Buffett recommend his own stock. The only book you will find written by him is a compilation of his annual letters to shareholders, while others promise riches with day trading, futures, commodities, real estate, books, and seminars. Berkshire offers no such gimmicks.

You have seen, read, and heard about the gimmicks; the incredible money making stock market strategies, workshops to take you from zero to zillion, excessive short term trading, penny stocks, foreclosures, spin offs, bankruptcy, initial public offerings (IPO), turnarounds, buying a stock before it splits and then selling it after it splits, buying stocks before ex-dividend dates, market timing, leveraged options, how to think like a millionaire, how to control assets without ownership, tax strategies, and turn $1,300 into $1 million in three years.

Books, seminars, tapes, workshops, workbooks, testimonials all present these gimmicks. You've seen the ads. Double your money every two and one-half to 4 months by writing covered calls is one of my favorites. One company has even gone as far as creating a Wealth Institute, a way to chart your financial future while providing graduate level financial instruction.

If these gimmicks are so successful , why would they advertise them, why would they charge for them, and why wouldn't everyone else do the same thing? Why not just take all the Wealth Institute knowledge and become so wealthy that you create the world's largest foundation and give it all away for the betterment of the world?

A major brokerage firm just sent me an old favorite stock market gimmick, 'the dogs of the Dow'. Buy the 10 highest dividend-yielding stocks in the Dow then every year 'rebalance'. So every year you are buying, selling, transacting, and for this privilege you pay your broker 1.48 percent the first year and 1.23 percent each subsequent year. What they don't tell you, if you do this in a taxable account you get a tax invoice from your broker each year. Subtract another 3 percent each year for taxes. So this gimmick doesn't disclose friction costs.

With Berkshire, there are no gimmicks, no false advertising, no bravado, no letters of endorsement, no fund czar, no analysts, no brokers. Nobody is paid to sell you on Berkshire.

96 Value Added

To own Berkshire is to add value, pure and simple. What is investing if it isn't the pursuit of adding value? Most individual investors do not add value. Most of the financial industry does not add value. If there is one thing to learn from this book, it is this concept of value added.

Every individual investor and every financial 'professional' should take the Financial Hippocratic Oath. First, do no harm to your investments.

New physicians are given an oath of ethical professional behavior attributed to Hippocrates, a Greek physician, born 460 B.C., and known as the father of medicine. Hippocrates founded the beginning of scientific medicine by freeing medical study from the constraints of philosophical speculation and superstition. He was the first to say that disease wasn't miraculous, and not a punishment from the gods.

The Hippocratic Oath is about a code of duty, honor, and professional ethics. It is about helping the unfortunate and abstaining from all intentional wrongdoing and harm.

We all should raise our right hands and repeat the Financial Hippocratic Oath:

(1) First, do no harm to your portfolio's returns.

(2) Always act in a way that adds value.

(3) Help those who are less financially astute.

(4) Taxes paid and under-performance are gone forever and compounded.

(5) Leave your finances in better shape whenever you make a financial decision.

(6) Compare your results against a fair benchmark.

(7) Bring light where there is darkness.

(8) Hire 'professionals' cautiously holding them to the same commandments.

(9) Fire any and all 'professionals' who do not add value.

(10) Always seek and speak the financial truth.

Have you ever billed someone for work that you didn't really add value to? It doesn't feel good to not be proud of your work. We feel good when we can contribute and offer a service or product that is value added and this is true for our individual finances as well as everything else in life.

For some strange reason the average individual investor does not understand that taxes paid are gone forever. Poor rates of return are lost forever. But even more compelling, taxes paid and poor performance are compounded. Three dollars paid annually in taxes on a $100 investment represents $300 in 20 years at 15 percent compounded. Likewise, $2 in a poor annual performance represents $200 in 20 years. Value subtracted adds up fast.

Last year the average mutual fund would have charged the Berkshire shareholders $1½ billion in fees to produce 2 percentage points less than the S&P 500 Index and would have passed along a $3 billion tax bill to each shareholder. Talk about value subtracted.

Berkshire's management on the other hand charged a mere $4 per share or approximately $6 million in administrative fees to return almost twice the S&P 500 Index. And Berkshire picked up the $3 billion tax bill on behalf of its owners. That's $2,000 of tax per share. Talk about value added.

According to the Security & Exchange Commission (SEC), mutual fund shareholders paid $34 billion in taxes on their 1997 gains and another estimated $40 billion in taxes in 1998. Moreover, in the last five years, investors in diversified U.S. stock funds surrendered an average of 15 percent of their annual gains to taxes. It seems individual investors don't make the connection between fund performance and after tax returns. It's a pity.

What a shame to look from a distance and observe most financial participants thinking they are better off doing what they are doing. It is like asking the average golfer who believes he or she is an above average player and will selectively remember the good shots, the good scores, the good rounds, and the good years.

Yet, you have seen them play and you know they are no better than bogie golfers. Every shot, hole, game, course, season, career they are offered a guaranteed par (what the average professional will score) in the form of an index fund. More than 90 percent choose to go it alone for a worse net score.

To continue the golf analogy, only a few professionals can offer value added and consistently shoot below par and make a nice living on the tour. Unlike golf, financial participants may choose to hire and capture the skill and superior performance of the best net scorer. Berkshire owners have chosen to hire the best shot-maker.

Berkshire upholds the Financial Hippocratic Oath. Mr. Buffett and his management team probably created it. Berkshire will always represent value added.

97 Financial Education (Part 1)

B ecause this book is dedicated to financial education, I have divided this reason #97 into two parts. This I believe is the most important reason to own Berkshire.

Berkshire has taught me more about investing than any other source. Just consider this list of topics: business, owner-ship, ethics, management, compensation, stocks, the market, accounting, value, intelligent versus emotional investing, bargain hunting, friction costs, dividends, stock splits, share price, decade trading, finance, mergers, acquisitions, private business sales, intrinsic value, book value, deferred taxes and taxation.

Berkshire also is about financial aptitude, financial literacy, retirement, education, children, charity, motivation, discipline, humility, honesty, character, fun, wit, self-deprecation, 20 investment punches in a lifetime, inheritance, succession, synergy, partnership attitude, shareholder value and portfolio concentration.

In essence, Berkshire is about life, and Mr. Buffett is a master teacher. Everything I learned about Berkshire hits home because I did everything else first. You might say I am one of the Berkshire prodigal sons.

After attending private schools for elementary and secondary education, I was accepted in one of the best business schools in the country. I was exposed to some of the best minds regarding finance, marketing, oral and written communication, accounting, statistics, business law, ethics, international business, retailing, management and all the rest of the typical business courses.

But my business education was incomplete. In business school, I hadn't heard about Berkshire Hathaway, Warren Buffett, value investing, economic value added, and investment comparisons. I graduated with a business degree but knew little about financial and business education.

You will learn more from your ownership in Berkshire than any formal education, extensive reading, family, friends, or hanging out with the best business minds. And, if you so choose, this is the first education that will pay you to learn. Berkshire will teach you about new concepts in finance, accounting, taxation, investing, acquisitions, and allocation.

You will need to *unlearn* some widely held beliefs:

(1) The rich get better opportunities.
(2) You always get what you pay for.
(3) Your home is your greatest asset.
(4) More money will solve most financial problems.
(5) Taxes are inevitable.
(6) Get rich quick is possible.
(7) Buy luxuries first.
(8) Education, success, big salaries, and status guarantees financial literacy and aptitude.
(9) Diversification is good.
(10) Emotions raise financial intelligence.
(11) Talent and hard work is enough.
(12) You can trade for a living.

Berkshire, through its chairman's letters dispels these beliefs and gives you a new way of seeing. Most schools do not teach proper finance and investing methods. Teachers cannot teach what they do not know.

As part of our financial education we play short-term, high-turnover, stock market games. When our educators need a professional expert on financial education, they bring in local stock brokers, financial advisors, and security analysts.

Financial problems surface because of two reasons: fear and ignorance. We are not properly educated. With a world population of six billion, most are literate but only a small percentage are financially literate. Until we start teaching the Berkshire Investment Model, our students will graduate with no financial foundation.

The recent book, *Rich Dad, Poor Dad: What the Rich Teach Their Kids About Money That the Poor and Middle Class Do Not!*, points out that rich people acquire assets. The poor and middle class acquire liabilities, but think they are assets.

The book goes on to say we need to acquire a financial IQ: accounting, investing, understanding markets, and understanding taxes. Financial intelligence is having more options and financial aptitude is what you do with the money you make, how to keep people from taking it, how long you keep it, and how hard your money is working for you.

Berkshire teaches us all these things and lowers our investing risk through financial education. Berkshire isn't a risk if you love what it is, know what it is, and understand what it is.

Berkshire teaches us about taxes more than any other investment, book, course, or expert. You are taxed when you earn, spend, save, and die. Mr. Buffett is a very astute reader of the tax code and has structured Berkshire to minimize the tax burden on all owners.

The biggest problem with our financial industry is not the enormous amount of money the industry makes with friction costs. It isn't even the lack of disclosure of costs, fees and taxes. It's not the hidden compensation, the soft dollars, the quiet quarterly mutual fund deductions for management. It's not the clever products created to sell just about everything we don't need financially. It's not even the whole general practice of subtracting value for services rendered.

The biggest problem with our financial industry is the lack of investor education. There is little truth coming from a money motivated, sales-driven, and transaction-oriented world of finance. Financial ignorance is lawful prey. Our best hope is that business schools will begin to teach the Berkshire Investment Model. I hope that Berkshire shareholders stipulate all future owner designated contributions to educational institutions be contingent on teaching and exposing students to Berkshire.

The bad news is financial education is a lifelong study. The good news is you can get a free education at www.

berkshirehathaway.com or you can get paid to learn by owning Berkshire. Make no mistake, the Berkshire financial education is more valuable than the Berkshire financial rewards.

97 Financial Education (Part 2)

B erkshire combines confidence with financial education to solve most financial problems. Personal financial difficulties are usually the result of fear and ignorance. Berkshire takes the emotion out of the investment equation. Emotions lower financial intelligence. Berkshire uses financial knowledge to create more options than you would have on your own.

For most investors, taxes are the biggest expense, and they need to work until the middle of May to pay their tax bill. Yet few investors consider the tax consequences when reviewing their financial options. Some, through ignorance, choose inappropriate investments because they let taxes drive the decision; or they turn to their CPA's and financial advisors for their taxation education.

Most believe that more money is the cure for most financial difficulties. But financial hardship must first be cured through education. More money without proper knowledge will lead to greater problems.

Get rich quick beliefs are like quick weight-loss programs. It sounds good but losing 20 pounds in 20 days is not a long-term solution and will probably be detrimental to your health.

Because we are ignorant, we diversify. We think it's playing it safe to put our eggs in many baskets. No one would admit that diversification is really a lack of financial education. Financial

education is having more options, not less. It doesn't mean trying out every option. Less is more. Berkshire helps you concentrate your portfolio into just three widely respected companies
representing 62 percent of its marketable securities.

Glancing at the local bookstore on business, finance, and investment book titles, it occurred to me that every popular title is
covered by a Berkshire financial education. Here's a list of titles
Mr. Buffett could have written:

(1) *Retire Worry Free*
(2) *Rule Breakers, Rule Makers*
(3) *Net Worth*
(4) *Smart Guide to Making Wise Investments*
(5) *The Truth about Money*
(6) *Integrity Management*
(7) *Creating Wealth*
(8) *Debt Free*
(9) *Plan Smart, Retire Rich*
(10) *Wealth 101*
(11) *Die Rich and Tax Free*
(12) *How to Be Rich*
(13) *Preserving Family Wealth*
(14) *Idiots Guide to Managing Your Money*
(15) *Financial Peace*
(16) *Investing Smart*
(17) *Stocks for the Long Run*
(18) *Where Are the Customers' Yachts?*
(19) *Outsmarting Wall Street*
(20) *The Unemotional Investor*

You get the idea. Many investment books can be viewed as
summarizing the Berkshire investment philosophy, and this is
just the investment section. The same would be true of other
book titles on taxation, management, mergers, accounting, philosophy, philanthropy, psychology, trusts, foundations, inheritance, partnerships, labor, time management, and acquisitions.

Here are some other popular books Mr. Buffett could have
conceived if the titles were changed to:

(1) *How to Get Started in Electronic* Decade *Trading*
(2) One *Step to Financial Freedom*
(3) *Foolish Guide to Picking* Too Many *Stocks*
(4) *How* Not *to Buy Technology Stocks*
(5) *The Dividend Investor:* Uncle Sam's Favorite
(6) *Live Rich, Die* Rich
(7) *The* Billionaire *Next Door*
(8) *The Millionaire* in Your Own Home
(9) Decade *Trading 101*
(10) *How I Made* 30 Billion *in The Stock Market*
(11) Honest *Poker*
(12) *How* Not *to Time the Stock Market*
(13) Berkshire *Money Machine: Old and Incredible Strategies for Cash Flow and Wealth Enhancement*
(14) *Trading to* Lose
(15) *Sleeping Like a Baby: Investing in* Berkshire
(16) *Study Guide for* Decade *Trading For a Living*
(17) *Complete Guide to an* Onshore *Money Haven*
(18) *How to Make Millions, Protect Your Privacy, and Legally* Defer *Taxes*
(19) *A Complete Idiot's Guide to* Berkshire
(20) Old *Market Timing Techniques: Why They* Won't *Work*

I would never suggest that any investment book or seminar be ignored. But once you have been educated in the Berkshire method, over half of what you read and hear will run contrary to your new beliefs. If every investor knew what Berkshire has taught those who take the time to learn, then everyone would invest in Berkshire. The secret to investment success is to have weak competition. If everyone does the same thing, we all get the same results.

Our best asset is our mind, and a financial education is one of the best gifts we can give ourselves. It must be sought from within.

One of my favorite books is *Think and Grow Rich* by Napoleon Hill. This book awakens your financial intelligence and genius. This book and the Berkshire Annual Reports are an inspiration.

I always wondered why they called the graduation ceremony from school "the commencement." Why would the end of such a long period of schooling be the beginning? I always thought of it as the end. To graduate was the goal, the end of the line, the diploma—the finish.

Now I realize that the end of my formal education was the beginning of my financial education. I don't expect to ever get a Berkshire diploma. I don't ever want to get a certification of my end of studying the greatest investment education in the world.

98 Investment Model (Part 1)

Berkshire, if it isn't already, will become the most sought after investment model. It will be taught in schools throughout the world. Normal finance 101 language will be circle of competence, margin of safety, intrinsic value, float, long-term, investing mistakes, no stock splits, book value, friction costs, and present value of a stream of earnings.

The Berkshire Investment Model is simple. Buy a few widely respected companies and to death do you part. It helps to have a management you respect, and loyal shareholders. It helps to have the most brilliant manager at the controls. It helps to buy in early and ride for a long time. Early owners of Berkshire had an easy decision to make. Once you've held Berkshire for eight and one-half years, your holdings multiplied ten times and selling didn't make much sense because of capital gain taxes and no better investment alternatives.

For those that have tried, it is difficult to put together the Berkshire Investment Model for textbooks and instructor outlines to be written. I have a course outline on the subject of Berkshire written.

I would recommend Berkshire 101 to someone, like myself, who made all the investing mistakes first and admitted them. Like running for President, this course is probably best for someone over 35 years of age, which means the average mutual fund manager wouldn't qualify.

I wish Berkshire 101 had been available to me when I was getting my degree in business administration, but in retrospect I wouldn't have gotten it. A certain amount of experience is required to understand Berkshire beliefs. Berkshire has benefited by institutions of higher learning teaching the wrong stuff, and by institutions giving finance degrees without a careful study and understanding of the Berkshire Investment Model. Even if students don't get it, I would still recommend exposure to Warren Buffett.

Text books for Berkshire 101 would be the Chairman's letters, *The Essays of Warren Buffett: Lessons for Corporate America* by Lawrence Cunningham, transcripts from the annual meetings, transcripts from Charlie Munger's speeches, and current books written about Mr. Buffett. *Intelligent Investor* and *Security Analysis* by Benjamin Graham would also be required reading.

I would like to point out that this is part of the "how" of Berkshire, which runs contrary to my belief to concentrate on the "why" of Berkshire.

The following is my textbook/course outline.

Berkshire Hathaway Investment Model:

    I.   The Berkshire Hathaway Story
    II.   Comparison To Other Models
    III.   Indexing
    IV.   Financial Analysis
    V.   Advanced Economics
    VI.   Advanced Accounting
    VII.   Value
    VIII.   Investing
    IX.   Capital Allocation
    X.   Trading
    XI.   Mergers and Acquisitions
    XII.   Taxation

XIII. Management Psychology
XIV. Management Motivation
 XV. Shareholder Management
XVI. Giving Back

Case Studies:

1. Acquiring a Whole Business
2. Acquiring Part of a Business
3. Acquiring Part Then the Whole Business

98 Investment Model (Part 2)

The following is the expanded tree branch of my attempt to define and outline the Berkshire investment method.

Berkshire Hathaway Investment Model:

  I. The Berkshire Hathaway Story
    A. History
    B. Buying a whole business (80–100 percent)
    C. Owning parts of a business (0–20 percent)
  II. Comparison to Other Models
    A. Identify other models
      1. momentum
      2. growth
      3. balanced
      4. high turnover
      5. sector
      6. value

B. Ability to read people
C. Manage the media
D. Moral and ethical standards
E. Operate inside the lines
F. Partnership attitude
XIV. Management Motivation
    A. Manager recognition
    B. Motivating wealthy managers
    C. Compensation
    D. Stock options
    E. Labor relations
    F. Retiree benefits
    G. X-factor: making Mr. Buffett proud
    H. The other half of the chairman's job
XV. Shareholder Management
    A. Lower investors' expectations
    B. Set an achievable goal
    C. Loyalty
    D. Owners manual
    E. Discounts
    F. Partnership attitude
    G. Board of directors
    H. Succession
    I. Attracting the best
    J. Annual meeting
    K. Annual report
    L. Quarterly earnings notice
    M. Media management
    N. Dividend policy
    O. Class A versus Class B shares
    P. Chairman's letter
XVI. Giving Back
    A. Owner designated
    B. Higher purpose
    C. Value of tax deferment
    D. Gift and estate transfer strategies
    E. New cost basis

F. World's largest foundation
G. Philanthropic thoughts
H. Return more claim checks than you take

Case Studies

1. Acquiring a Whole Business
   A. See's Candies
   B. Buffalo News
   C. GenRe
2. Acquiring Part of a Business
   A. Coke
   B. Washington Post
   C. Gillette
3. Acquiring Part Then the Whole Business
   A. GEICO

99 For All Seasons

Berkshire is an investment for all financial seasons. It's the most fertile land with the best fertilizer in the spring. It's the shade during the hot summer. It's the bountiful harvest in the fall. But most important, it's the umbrella during the rain, the skis and sled to navigate through the snow and a solid storm shelter during any tornado, hurricane or typhoon.

Berkshire has the most advanced satellite coverage combined with the best weather forecaster—always looking forward ten years. The weather affects the forecaster greater than those he is reporting to so he has a strong incentive to get it right.

There are two types of seasons with which an investor should be concerned. The first type of season is inward (personal), the second outward (markets and salesmen).

Berkshire is suited for all the personal financial seasons from birth, to life, to death, and beyond. Berkshire is your answer to funding a child's education, building a financial nest egg, planning for retirement, preserving family wealth, gifting to beneficiaries, and providing for a long-term foundation for the betterment of society.

Berkshire is the investment of choice for lottery winnings, to dollar cost averaging, to a child's first stock, for the proceeds of a small business sale, and for any large or small settlement. This wonderful investment choice will best preserve short bursts of income, a long steady small stream or a lump sum retirement.

Berkshire is a wonderful place to be if you happen to be a media or sports celebrity. An entertainer's challenge is how to handle enormous amounts of money in a short period of time, without falling prey to the 'professional' financial advisors.

As to the second outward season, Berkshire is the proven master of all markets. It's a constant market out-performer in prosperous times, but more important, has never lost money— even in the worst of times.

Most investors think there are only two market seasons: a bull market where equities rise over time or a bear market where equities trend lower. How long each market environment lasts is anyone's guess. The financial seasons change quickly without notice.

There are more seasons than bull or bear markets. There's a time to be in cash waiting for better values. There's a time to acquire a whole business. There's a time to own part of a business. There's a time to be in bonds. There's a time to be in preferred stocks. There's a time to be in certain equity sectors. There's even a season to be in commodities and Berkshire's chairman monitored and waited for this season for over 40 years before he purchased 20 percent of the world's silver supply.

Sometimes there's a long season to be in equities, known as "The Inevitables:" stocks you can hold forever, like Coke, Gillette, and the most obvious inevitable, Berkshire itself.

Sometimes there's a season and fertile land only available to companies like Berkshire. Convertible preferred stock that pays a special dividend with a special conversion feature. Whenever or if ever the common stock is more attractive, Berkshire has been allowed to convert into the more favorable investment when the seasons changed.

With such a large global lifeboat, Berkshire is the first stopping point for anyone looking for rescue. And as a result can be very choosy as to what, when, and where it lets in.

So whatever the season in your personal life or whatever the season in the world marketplace, Berkshire is the best financial silver bullet, the best choice for your family's wealth. One choice prepares you for any season.

100 State of Mind

Berkshire is a state of mind. Berkshire is a life-style. Berkshire encompasses your whole being. Berkshire is here, there, everywhere. Berkshire is one billion daily servings of Coke generating $33,333 in Berkshire hourly earnings. Berkshire is your local Dairy Queen, your daily whiskers, your home mortgage, even your auto insurance. It's the candy you eat, encyclopedias your children read, shoes and jewelry you wear, and news from our nation's capital.

Berkshire is like being an entrepreneur. It redefines you. It becomes you. It represents you. To be an entrepreneur is to live a certain way: To create resources where none existed, to embrace risk, to live in such a way that opportunities constantly present themselves. An enterprising personality is always looking to fulfill needs in the marketplace. An entrepreneur's mind is never at rest.

Berkshire is a thought process. To think like an owner and to think long-term in a short-term oriented world.

Berkshire is a way of life. It's living below your means no matter how little or great your means are. Berkshire is about work and to have meaningful work or a personal mission that makes you tap dance.

In the East they have a concept called Dharma: to do that which you have been born to do. Some people have a Dharma to teach, some to create art, some to restore old cars. Others are born to make people laugh; even more to help others in need. Whatever your Dharma, Berkshire is about achieving that state of being.

Fortunately for shareholders, Mr. Buffett's Dharma is to buy whole and parts of a business at a good value and motivate a well-compensated management team to continue growing the business.

- Berkshire is a moral code, it's about character. Character is built over a lifetime and destroyed in a few minutes without proper guidelines to follow. Berkshire is about working with people you enjoy and respect, and to never put yourself in a position that would compromise your character.
- Berkshire is about adding value; to add value or not be part of the equation. If you are not contributing, replace yourself with someone who can make a greater contribution.
- Berkshire is about leadership; to do the right thing, to choose the path less traveled, to be contrarian.
- Berkshire is about results; superior performance without ever losing money.
- Berkshire is about humility; to constantly lower expectations, to never advertise, to never recommend itself to others. It is unassuming. Promise less and deliver more.
- Berkshire is about synergy; to make acquisitions that add value to the whole company and reciprocally to have the resources of the parent company's capital for expansion of a subsidiary.

- Berkshire is an attitude; to contribute more than you take. It's about civic pride and local values. Berkshire is about charity, helping where your heart is warmed.
- Berkshire is about minimizing your investments and possessions and simplifying your life.
- Berkshire is an intellectual and emotional challenge. Keep in check your feelings of being better and smarter than most, and your emotions of fear, greed, and get rich quick. It's about using your head, not your heart, to make economic decisions.
- Berkshire is about living your daily life. It's about preserving your family's wealth and values. Berkshire is your approach. It's how you start and finish.
- Berkshire is about macro-management; giving your life savings to a proven concept united with a proven manager and then letting him do his job. Berkshire doesn't peek over the shoulders of its operating managers, nor does it attempt to fix all problems. Generally, Berkshire first allocates excess capital generated by its wholly owned subsidiaries, and secondly, motivates its managers to do a better job than you or I would do.
- Berkshire can make you a better person; confident, virtuous, more of a capitalist. It makes you less of a believer in the lottery mentality: a huge payoff with little or no risk of capital and time.

Berkshire is like the old American tale, *The Wizard of Oz*. The Wizard of Wall Street isn't at Wall Street or Kansas, but in Nebraska. To find your goal, you follow the yellow Berk road. You may be seeking home, heart, courage, or intelligence and you may pick up some like-minded friends along the way. No path is without distraction and evil forces trying to turn you back.

You might find you don't need the man behind the curtain in Berkshire City to extol your qualities. When you leave home thinking that riches and opportunities are only to be found elsewhere, you may be surprised they are here at home. Your journey can begin and end right where you start.

101 Simplicity

B erkshire is simple and pure. Like a great athlete, Mr. Buffet makes the investment process look effortless, graceful and deceptively easy. Greatness in any endeavor can be defined by how easy the task appears. Greatness leads others to temptation.

That which is simplest is easiest to maintain. Complex requires reinforcements, back up, energy, tiers, insurance, justification, maintenance, fees, consultants, architects, engineers, accountants, salesmen, attorneys, the works. Complexity requires your time and with your investments your money.

Only time will prove complex or simple. You won't know which is correct until many years doing the same complex or simple method.

Ray Kroc, founder of McDonald's, made the concept of K.I.S.S. famous; Keep It SIMPLE Stupid. His restaurant chain has become widely respected because of its simplicity.

Most investment 'professionals' make the investment process far more complicated than necessary, probably to justify themselves and their fees. The investment process is really about asset allocation, in which diversification is assumed, appreciated, and greatly compensated.

Even individual investors, left to their own decisions, universally choose complication; a hodgepodge of assorted mutual funds, individual stocks, annuities, insurance products, bonds, commodities, options, trusts, partnerships, assorted accounts titled this way and that. There is a perceived safety in complication, diversification, and disorder.

It's a rare individual who indexes for simplicity. Since there's no money in it, it's even rarer to find a financial 'professional' who recommends indexing your investments.

Berkshire is simpler than indexing. To index is to diversify, to choose large cap, small cap, international, Pacific, Europe, growth, value, balanced, sector, mid cap, technology, short/mid/long term bonds, or cash.

As we become successful, we are led to believe that success means greater complexity. More choices can lead to greater difficulty and more decisions.

At the other extreme, acts of financial desperation always lead to greater complexity. Get rich quick schemes are never simple. Complexity and simplicity are both choices. To choose complex financial affairs is a choice, consciously or unconsciously, to compete against Berkshire.

Have you ever noticed how investment books, seminars, newsletters, and telemarketing proposals are complicated? Complex means diversification. Even though value is always compromised when quantity takes precedence over quality. To diversify is to do what everyone else does so you'll get the same results as everyone else.

Simplicity is to own one security that owns 100 different companies plus a smaller percentage of seven widely respected and publicly traded companies. It's not easy to be an expert at more than a handful of businesses.

Complexity is transaction intensive and tax complicated. Complexity followers are likely to describe their results as comparatively pretty good or above average. It's like asking a parent or grandparent how intelligent their child is. Most if not all will tell you how smart their children are, sometimes without you asking them. But how many teachers pull parents aside and say their child is a genius or above average?

Berkshire simplifies your taxes—there are none. Complex investment models require complex tax payments. The most complicated tax shelter I ever purchased—where for every dollar you pay you get two dollars back on your taxes—never lived up to its billing, and I couldn't do my own taxes. I never really understood it. Talk about subtracting value. They even asked for additional contributions after losing my money.

Berkshire simplifies your reporting with one annual report.

Berkshire simplifies your monthly statements. If you take possession of your stock certificates, which Class A share holders must to participate in the owner-designated charity program, you won't get monthly statements.

Berkshire simplifies your investment comparisons—if it continues to beat the S&P 500 Index continue to own it. If it doesn't beat the index, find something that does or own the index itself. Manage Berkshire like Berkshire manages its operating companies. Review quarterly reports and carefully read the annual report. To death do you part.

There are more Warren Wannabes than Berkshire shareholders and most want to know how Mr. Buffett performs his investment magic. It doesn't matter to the faithful loyal shareholder. The long-term Berkshire shareholder will not do anything different if interest rates go up or down, if a new initial public offering is announced, if technology makes an inevitable major change, if the Dow drops 25 percent, if the Chairman of the Federal Reserve makes a major announcement, or the Middle East becomes a war zone. It doesn't matter because the long-term shareholder has chosen simplicity.

No need to monitor the markets or even watch the daily prices of Berkshire or its publicly traded components. Cancel your subscriptions to all the financial publications. It's that simple.

If 92 percent of your investment returns are due to capital allocation, why not allocate 92 percent of your portfolio to the best capital allocator in the business?

Berkshire is simple but not very easy. Just take another peek at Reason #98 the Berkshire Investment Model.

Another way to spell Berkshire is S.I.M.P.L.E.

S = Shareholders are always first at Berkshire.

I = Intelligent Investing. May also represent the Inevitables.

M = Mr. Market (emotional investing) antidote.

P = Proven, Professional, Performer, also Promises kept.

L = Life-style, Leadership, Longevity, Low taxes, Leverage (float), Look through earnings.

E = Everlasting, Extraordinary Earnings, Experience.

Berkshire is simplification. Choose Berkshire and simplify your choices and decisions. You really need to make two decisions to manage your investments. First, make Berkshire your largest holding. Second, never forget your first decision.

Conclusion

There you have it. *101 Reasons To Own the World's Greatest Investment.* Even if you decide not to own Berkshire, this book should help you look at investments and advisors in a new way.

It took 30 years of doing everything else first before I found Berkshire. I have shared my experiences to help you reach your goal much faster.

Remember, this list contains reasons to OWN Berkshire, not trade, short, option, shadow, compete, second guess, or daily monitor Berkshire. Ownership has rewards few will ever appreciate if there's only a short-term orientation.

Speaking of short term, I have just finished reading the Coca Cola annual report and I was struck by how the chairman had to spend most of his letter pleading to shareholders to look beyond a 1.4 percent annual return for 1998. A widely respected company whose market value has increased from $16 billion to $165 billion in the past 10 years is apologizing for a short term under performance due to world economic difficulties.

When will we get it? A lumpy 26 percent average annual return is better than a smooth 12 percent return. As Mr. Ivester, the former Chairman of Coke, said, "Troubled markets will improve. And people will still get thirsty."

The concept of this book is based upon why you should own Berkshire, not how. Competing against Berkshire is futile. Remember we are all victims of a lack of financial education and inertia. We are all likely to keep doing what we have been doing because of the energy it takes to change investment strategies and courses. I hope you choose the Berkshire solution, and that I see you at the annual meeting.

Once again I am not and have never been employed by the financial industry, the financial media, Berkshire Hathaway, any subsidiary, and or partly owned business. I am not trained or certified to give financial, tax, legal, personal, or investment advice. My writings reflect a perspective of a private investor, small businessman, and lifelong student of investing. I have casually met Mr. Buffett and Mr. Munger but have not been selected by them to undertake this project. I have absolutely nothing to gain or lose if you buy, sell, shadow, observe, short, or ignore this wonderful company.

However, I do have something to gain as a long term shareholder, if you decide to sell your business (if it meets the acquisition criteria) to Berkshire as a result of reading this book, Berkshire becomes an ever-expanding world's greatest investment.

It's not my intention to be or become a financial guru, widely quoted expert, talking head or pundit. But I hope you join me in my admiration of Mr. Buffett and Mr. Munger, and observe, and admire what they have accomplished. Then, you will be convinced as I have.

I have been attracted to this company because they created a home for investors like me. They have welcomed me with open arms, and I have never been anywhere, like Omaha, where so many are trying to shadow and compete with the best of the best.

I didn't undertake this project to make money but to share what I have learned. I have already gotten the best compensation that any writer would hope for: a better understanding of the subject, respect from intelligent minds, and responses from other members of the Motley Fool Internet message board that warm my heart.

I have written with candor but not with ill will. I have taken issue with most of the financial industry, the financial press, and day traders. My work may well be unknown and my ideas and character have been and will be attacked. This is a small price to pay to speak the truth. I offer my apologies to those that I have offended. I never intended to attack anyone's character.

Hopefully, one day, you will find a company like Berkshire Hathaway that you will want to own for life. It will be a company that will endure and profit regardless of what is happening in the ever-changing, turbulent world economy.

One hundred and one reasons sounded easy to do but thinking and debating one hundred and one reasons to do anything is a challenge. As someone said, most people can come up with two reasons to justify a stock purchase. One, the stock has gone up, and two, it's likely to go up more before they sell it.

I hope you choose to own Berkshire after careful consideration and that as like minds we meet one day—maybe one spring weekend in Omaha.

Appendix I

Twenty-five Questions Every Wise Investor Should Ask

By asking the right questions, you may leap from a beginner to a wise investor in a single bound. Asking the right questions is the start of a financial education, because if you don't know the right questions, how will you know the right answers?

(1) How does my investment return compare, net of all costs and taxes?

(2) What is a proper comparison index?

(3) What is passive investment management?

(4) Is active management better than passive management?

(5) If not me, who is the best at managing my money?

(6) How do I recognize true investment talent?

(7) How much does this talent cost?

(8) What can I learn from my mistakes?

(9) What can I learn from this new method of investing?

(10) Can I hire him/her?

(11) Is there a public record of performance?

(12) Does the past performance belong to another manager?

(13) What can I read and learn?

(14) Is there a meeting I can attend to find out more?

(15) Do they advertise? Do they recommend their own stock?

(16) Who recommends it?

(17) What do the analysts say?

(18) What does the financial media say?

(19) How is it rated by investment advisory services?

(20) Who else owns it?

(21) Where can I find other investors who think like me?

(22) Do I qualify? What is the minimum investment?

(23) Is there an owner's manual I can read before I invest?

(24) Have I ever read anything about this investment that I don't believe?

(25) How is the manager compensated?

Appendix II
Twenty Investment Punches

M r. Buffett suggests that each investor get just 20 invest-ment moves in a lifetime. It amazing that some of us would use up our allotment within one day of trading. Here's what my investment punch list would look like. What would yours look like?

○ 1. Bought Greyhound Bus Lines
○ 2. Sold Greyhound Bus Lines
○ 3. Bought first mutual fund
○ 4. Bought and sold stock options
○ 5. Invested with no cost student loans
○ 6. Bought and sold equities
○ 7. Bought and sold gold coins
○ 8. Bought and sold futures
○ 9. Bought and sold hottest momentum funds
○ 10. Bought too many mutual funds
○ 11. Hired first money manager
○ 12. Hired too many money managers
○ 13. Fired first money manager
○ 14. Hired consultant to find best money manager
○ 15. Discovered index investing
○ 16. Fired the rest of the money managers
○ 17. Sold all mutual funds
○ 18. Bought tech stocks

○ 19. Bought and sold tech stock options and puts
○ 20. Bought Berkshire Hathaway

Now I am out of punches. How many punches did it or will it take you to own Berkshire Hathaway?

Appendix III

Eight Ways We Become Investment Victims

The following is why I think most of us are victims of our current but changing investment environment. Websites like *www.vanguard.com* and *www.fool.com* are beginning to help teach, inform, entertain, and amuse the vast population of financial victims.

1. A Lack Of Financial Education: First and foremost we are all victims by not having the right financial education. We graduate elementary, secondary, college, and in my case business school without really knowing anything about the world of finance and investments. We are left at the mercy of self-interested parties to teach us what we don't know. Unfortunately those left to teach have incentives to not educate us. We are not taught to compare. We are not taught what alternatives are available. We are not given proper reports listing results with a proper benchmark. We have no idea what we are invested in and how much we are paying. We aren't given the right answers because we don't know the right questions. We are often given the wrong answers to the right questions and are given the wrong answers to the wrong questions. Most know that their brokers are not completely honest but don't know where else to turn.

When teachers attempt to teach elementary students the basics about investing they bring in the 'professionals' to teach the wrong stuff. When teachers think they are helping our youngsters, they introduce them to day trading in the form of a contest that emphasizes technology, Internet, and short term trading. We are providing our children with the wrong financial curriculum.

Even well-meaning parents make mistakes. If parents, the most critical ingredient to a child's education, are part of the 95 percent of short-term traders, our children don't have a chance.

Two concepts foreign to all students—even the most aspiring business school students—are the concept of ownership and the concept of concentration.

We need to take the financial education process out of the hands of interested parties and expose it to everyone based on objectivity and truth. One of the best books to address this problem is *Rich Dad Poor Dad: What the Rich Teach Their Kids About Money—That the Poor and Middle Class Do Not!* written by Robert T. Kiyosaki and Sharon L. Lechter.

Everything starts and ends with financial education. Even people, who think they are wise, fall prey to thinking they know what they think is right. Some poor souls have the right answers to the wrong questions. How many people like me need 30 years of financial illiteracy to finally become financially literate?

You should teach your children:

(1) Ninety-two percent of your investment return is determined by asset allocation.

(2) If you choose to hire someone to help you with your investments he or she generally will charge more for adding less.

(3) All investments need to be compared to an index. If they beat the index, continue to hold; if they fail, then sell.

(4) Most fees in the financial world are hidden.

(5) Read annual reports from the back to the front. It is what they don't tell you that is important.

(6) Very, very few individuals have true investment talent.

(7) Learn everything you can about indexing.

(8) Know what questions to ask.

(9) It is what you don't know that can hurt you.

(10) If you do what everyone else is doing you will get the same results as everyone else.

(11) Ownership is long term.

(12) Loyalty is rewarded.

(13) Friction costs will take away five percent annually from your returns.

(14) Wealth creation is a long-term affair.

(15) Focus on buying assets, not liabilities that you think are assets.

2. *Inertia*: What we have been doing is what we are likely to continue to do in the future. We usually justify whatever we have done or are in the process of doing. Its takes a secure person to say, "What I've been doing is wrong."

Once we make an investment decision we are usually frozen because of the tax consequences if we change. Some would like to switch horses but despise paying taxes more than being on the right horse.

Others don't know or don't care that they're on the wrong horse. They aren't aware that there is even a race and they are losing at every turn; annually two percent for transaction costs, three percent for taxes, and three percent for inflation. That's eight percent every year.

Many investors don't really care as long as we are in a long bull market. When you are getting 20 percent returns, who cares about the hidden costs? Let's just keep doing what we're doing.

Change requires effort, time, comparisons, thought, analysis, and work. Inertia doesn't require anything. That which starts in motion stays in motion until it meets an opposite force of equal or greater energy. Do you have the time, energy, and interest to make the appropriate changes?

3. *Ego*: The more successful we become the more likely our ego drives us to think we must be good at everything. The logic is there. If we excel in other aspects of our lives then certainly we can excel at investments.

It is said that doctors are notorious at making bad investments. Why would a smart individual be so bad at such a simple thing like investments? Part of it is ego. If they are smart enough to save a human life with the most complicated surgical techniques, then they certainly should be able to understand wise investments and make the right choices. Investments are indeed another science, but the part most of us miss is that it's also an art and there are very few master investment painters.

Also I think doctors are targets for the financial industry. They cannot do their own brain surgery so they automatically go to the investment doctor.

I don't mean to pick on doctors because the rest of us are just as vulnerable to our own egos. It's the rare person who says he or she is not good at everything. They just focus on what they are good at and turn their finances over to an index fund or something better.

The test is simple. If your investments have beaten the S&P Index over the last five years or greater then keep doing what you're doing. If they haven't or you don't know, then you may be a victim of ego.

4. *Taxes*: The government loves day traders. The government loves 95 percent of most 'investors'. The IRS is their silent partner with the average NASDAQ 'owner' turning over their holdings every six months.

The tax collectors love mutual funds. Not only do they charge you hidden fees, but they Velcro tax invoices on you with annual capital gain distributions whether they have added value or not. Your friendly mutual fund reports everything to the government each year. For the privilege of a mutual fund providing less value, they also deliver an annual tax bill to every investor.

When are we going to understand the tax consequence behind our investment choices? Long term investors, the rare true owners, should hope that tax legislation doesn't change to discourage short term trading. Just think what would happen if there were no capital gain taxes after holding an investment for 20 years? There are many ways to beat taxes. The best way is to own a security that doesn't pay dividends and holds them long term.

Money you pay in taxes is money that is gone forever.

5. *No Comparison*: How do we know if our investments are providing bad, good, average, or superior performance? Why don't brokerage statements include simple comparisons? Why don't brokerage statements show cost basis for each asset held vs market price? Why don't brokerage statements show unrealized and realized gains and losses? Why don't brokerage statements show a portfolio's net return compared to an appropriated weighted index?

Why don't mutual fund statements and advertisements show results as compared to an appropriate index? Why don't mutual funds report costs, fees, and tax consequences in large type in the beginning? Why do 'investors' put up with such treatment?

If I were to start a mutual fund I would start 50 different portfolios. Then I would take the best performer after one year and pour the other 49 portfolios into it. I would advertise the out performer like crazy. I would build assets under management quickly. I would make the future results difficult to compare. And this would all be perfectly legal.

We are victims of no simple comparison of results, costs, fees, and taxes. Do you really know if you or your chosen experts have added value?

6. *Justification*: No matter that we can justify everything we do, even poor investment results. It's part of our nature. It takes a very secure person to say that which I've done is wrong. I need to change my investment approach.

7. *Improper Information*: If we are not given the right information we are not properly informed. If we don't know the right questions we can't get the right answers.

8. *Optimism*: In a recent poll by consulting firm KPMG of New York, three out of four college students expect to become millionaires. That's optimism. Especially when you consider that less than two percent of the population has reached this financial goal.

We're optimistic by nature and it's a good thing unless we're talking about our investments. To be too optimistic about one's investing talent can be costly.

In Mr. Buffett's 1989 letter to shareholders he talked about the 'institutional imperative'. He defines this behavior as; one, institutions resist change; two, institutions find investments to soak up available funds; three, foolish investing will be supported by data, and four, institutional peers will mindlessly imitate one another.

Just as there's an 'institutional imperative' there is also an 'individual investor imperative'. An individual by nature resists change. Our investments will expand to soak up available dollars. Foolish investing will always be supported by data, by blindness, or by ignorance and investors big or small are very much lemming like, mindlessly imitating one another.

Appendix IV

Investment Beliefs and Philosophies

Most investors haphazardly assemble a portfolio without careful consideration to an overall investment philosophy. Why not turn it around and develop investment philosophies then find an investment that fits your beliefs. Here are my investment beliefs and philosophies. Maybe by reviewing these you can see how Berkshire matches my beliefs.

(1) There are very, very few individuals who add value to your individual investments.

(2) Hire the best investment manager.

(3) Low costs matter.

(4) Low taxes matter.

(5) Low portfolio turnover matters.

(6) Make sure the investment manager has your best interests in his heart.

(7) Keep it simple (be able to explain your investment program to a 10 year old).

(8) Buy and hold (long term).

(9) Buy equities (100 percent).

(10) Hold individual stock certificates.

(11) Invest in a stock built to last.

(12) Eliminate emotion from investing.

(13) Stay within your circle of competence.

(14) Concentrate your holdings into a few quality world class companies.

(15) Give back.

(16) Investing is a part of life and a lifelong endeavor.

(17) Investing is not as complicated or as simple as it looks.

(18) Be patient.

(19) Investments in motion tend to stay in motion; we are victims of investing inertia.

(20) Most investors have a genuine dislike for taxes.

(21) Dollar cost averaging works.

(22) Reduce investing mistakes.

(23) Delay gratification.

(24) Understand the importance of passive (index) investing.

Appendix V

Recommended Free Web Sites

www.berkshirehathaway.com .. official Web site, annual reports and chairman's letters

www.bigcharts.com .... charts, comparison

www.bloomberg.com .... research and financial news

www.businessweek.com....... research and financial news

www.cnbc.com.............. research and financial news

www.cnnfn.com............. research and financial news

www.focusinvestor.com .... unofficial Berkshire Hathaway Web site

www.fool.com .... financial news, advice, and discussion groups

www.forbes.com............. research and financial news

www.fortune.com............ research and financial news

http://investor.msn.com .... research and financial news

www.kiplinger.com.......... research and financial news

www.money.com .... research and financial news

www.morningstar.com .... research and financial news

www.sec.gov................ EDGAR database

www.smartmoney.com........ research and financial news

www.ticonline.com........... unofficial Web site for all things related to Berkshire Hathaway

www.vanguard.com . . . . research and financial
education
www.worth.com . . . . research and financial news

Top Investment Web Sites

www.cnnfn.com . . . . research and financial news
http://cbs.marketwatch.com . . . . research and financial news
www.ft.com . . . . research and financial news
www.hoovers.com . . . . research
www.investorguide.com . . . . research
www.investorhome.com . . . . research
www.investors.com . . . . Investor's Business Daily
http://moneycentral.com . . . . . . research
www.morningstar.com . . . . research
www.msnbc.com . . . . research and financial news
www.nbr.com . . . . PBS Nightly Business Report
www.nytimes.com . . . . research and financial news
www.personalwealth.com . . . . . S&P
www.quicken.com . . . . research
http://quote.yahoo.com . . . . research and financial news
www.usatoday.com/money/
mfront/htm . . . . research and financial news

Investment Web Sites Designed for Younger Investors

www.betterinvesting.org/youth/youth.html
www.fool.com/teens/familycollection/980325.htm
www.irs.gov/taxi/

www.kidmoney.org
library.thinkquest.org/3088 . . . .(stock market education)
library.thinkquest.org/3298 . . . .(investing in your future)
library.thinkquest.org/3096 . . . .(by kids, for kids)
www.moneyoplis.org
www.theyoungamericans.org/
www.treas.gov/opc/opc0034.html . .(FAQ U.S. paper currency)
www.wsjclassroomedition.com/wsj_teencenter.htm
www.ustreas.gov/kids/

'Unofficial' Web Site to Calculate Berkshire Hathaway's Intrinsic Value

http://creativeacademics.com/finance/iv.html

Web Site for 'Unofficial' Berkshire Hathaway Frequently Asked Questions

http://boards.fool.com/message.asp?mid=13661234

Appendix VI

Recommended Berkshire Hathaway-Related Books and Web Sites

Berkshire Hathaway: The Ultimate Conglomerate Discount, Local Paine Webber Office, Alice Schroeder, Insurance Analyst, Jan. 1999.

Benjamin Graham on Value Investing, Janet Lowe, Penguin, 1996.

Buffett: The Making of an American Capitalist, Roger Lowenstein, Doubleday, 1996.

Damn Right: Behind the Scenes with Berkshire-Hathaway Billionaire Charlie Munger, Janet Lowe, John Wiley & Sons, Inc., 2000.

The Essays Of Warren Buffett: Lessons for Corporate America, Lawrence Cunningham, The Cunningham Group, 1998.

How to Pick Stocks Like Warren Buffett, Timothy Vick, McGraw-Hill, 2000.

The Intelligent Investor: A Book of Practical Counsel, Benjamin Graham, HarperCollins, Revised Edition, 1997.

Of Permanent Value: The Story of Warren Buffett/Monster Millennium Edition, Andrew Kilpatrick, AKPE, 2000.

The Rediscovered Benjamin Graham, Janet Lowe, John Wiley & Sons, Inc., 1999.

Security Analysis, Benjamin Graham & David Dodd, McGraw-Hill, 1996.

Thoughts of Chairman Buffett: Thirty Years of Unconventional Wisdom from The Sage of Omaha, Simon Reynolds, Harper Business, 1998.

Value Investing Made Easy, Janet Lowe, McGraw-Hill, 1997.

Wall Street on Sale, Timothy Vick, McGraw Hill, 1999.

The Warren Buffett Portfolio: Mastering The Power of The Focus Investment Strategy, Robert Hagstrom, John Wiley & Sons, Inc., 2000.

Warren Buffett Speaks: Wit and Wisdom from The World's Greatest Investor, Janet Lowe, John Wiley & Sons, Inc., 1997.

The Warren Buffett Way: Investment Strategies of the World's Greatest Investor, Robert Hagstrom, John Wiley & Sons, Inc., 1997.

Recommended Books for Young Investors

The Complete Idiot's Guide to Raising Money-Smart Kids, Barbara Weltman, Macmillan, 1999.

The Everything Kids' Money Book, Diane Mayr, Adams Business Media, 2000.

It's My Money: A Kid's Guide to the Green Stuff, Ann Banks, Penguin, 1993.

Kid Cash: Creative Money-Making Ideas, Joe Lamancusa, McGraw-Hill, 1993.

The Kid's Allowance Book, Amy Nathan, Walkers' Co., 1998.

Kid's Allowances—How Much, How Often & How Come, A Guide for Parents, David McCurrach, Kids Money Press, 2000.

Kids and Money: Giving Them the Savvy to Succeed Financially, Jayne Pearl, Bloomberg Press, 1999.

The Kid's Guide to Money: Earning It, Saving It, Spending It, Growing It, Sharing It, Steven Otfinoski, Scholastic, 1996.

Kids, Money & Values: Creative Ways to Teach Your Kids about Money, Patricia Estess, F&W Publications, 1994.

Kids, Parents & Money: Teaching Personal Finance from Piggy Bank to Prom, Willard & William Stawski, John Wiley & Sons, Inc., 2000.

Mom, Can I Have That?: Dr. Tightwad Answers Your Kids' Questions about Money, Janet Bodnar, Kiplinger Books, 1996.

Money Doesn't Grow on Trees: A Parent's Guide to Raising Financially Responsible Children, Neale Godfrey, Simon & Schuster, 1993.

Money Sense for Kids, Hollis Harman, Barrons Juveniles, 1999.

101 Marvelous Money-Making Ideas for Kids, Heather Wood, Tor Books, 1995.

A Penny Saved: Teaching Your Children the Values and Life-Skills They Will Need to Live in the Real World, Neale Godfrey, Simon & Schuster, 1996.

Smart-Money Moves for Kids, Judith Briles, Mile High Press, 2000.

The Totally Awesome Money Book for Kids (& Their Parents), Adriane Berg, Newmarket Press, 1993.

Berkshire Hathaway Subsidiary Companies Web Sites

Acme Building Brands . . . . .www.acmebuildingbrands.com

Adalet . . . . .www.adalet.com

Arbortech . . . . .www.arbortech.cc

Ben Bridge Jeweler . . . . .www.benbridge.com

Benjamin Moore . . . . .www.benjaminmoore.com

Berkshire Hathaway Group . . . . .www.brkdirect.com

Borsheim's Fine Jewelry . . . . . . .www.borsheims.com

Buffalo NEWS, Buffalo NY . . . . .www.buffnews.com
Campbell Hausfeld . . . . .www.chpower.com
Carefree of Colorado . . . . .www.digidot.com/carefree
Central States Indemnity . . . . . .www.csi-omaha.com
CORT Business Services www.cort1.com
Dexter Shoe Company . . . . .www.dextershoe.com
Douglas/Quikut . . . . .www.quikut.com
Executive Jet . . . . .www.netjets.com
Fechheimer Brothers Company . . .www.fechheimer.com
FlightSafety . . . . .www.flightsafety.com
France . . . . .www.franceformer.com
GEICO Direct Auto Insurance . . . .www.geico.com
General & Cologne Re Group . . . .www.genre.com
Halex . . . . .www.halexco.com
Helzberg Diamonds . . . . .www.helzberg.com
H.H. Brown Shoe Company . . . . .www.hhbrown.com
International Dairy Queen, Inc. . .www.dairyqueen.com
Jordan's Furniture . . . . .www.jordansfurniture.com
Justin Brands . . . . .www.justinboots.com
www.chippewaboots.com
www.nocona.com
www.tonylama.com
Kingston . . . . .www.kingstontimer.com
Kirby . . . . .www.kirby.com
Lowell Shoe Company www.comfort2u.com
Meriam Instrument . . . . .www.meriam.com
MidAmerican Energy . . . . .www.midamerican.com
National Indemnity Company . . .www.nationalindemnity.com
Nebraska Furniture Mart . . . . . .www.nfm.com
Northland . . . . .www.northlandmotor.com
Precision Steel Warehouse, Inc. . . .www.precisionsteel.com

RC Willey Home Furnishings . . . .www.rcwilley.com

Scot Laboratories . . . . .www.scotlabs.com

Scottcare . . . . .www.scottcare.com

Scott Fetzer Companies

See's Candies . . . . .www.sees.com

Shaw Industries . . . . .www.shawinc.com

Stahl .www.stahl.cc

Star Furniture . . . . .www.starfurniture.com

United States Liability . . . . .www.usli.com

Western Enterprises . . . . .www.westernenterprises.com

World Book . . . . .www.worldbook.com

Appendix VII

Copyright Notice

The following material is copyrighted by Warren E. Buffett and is reprinted here with written permission.

Reprinting any of this Appendix material without written permission may be a violation of copyright law.

Appendix VIII

Berkshire Hathaway's Owner's Manual

Berkshire Hathaway Inc.

Warren Buffett's 14 Owner-Related Business Principles

An Owner's Manual*
A Message from Warren E. Buffett
Chairman and CEO
January 1999

Introduction

Augmented by the General Re merger, Berkshire's shareholder count has doubled in the past year to about 250,000. Charlie Munger, Berkshire's Vice Chairman and my partner, and I welcome each of you. As a further greeting, we have prepared a second printing of this booklet to help you understand our business, goals, philosophy and limitations.

These pages are aimed at explaining our broad principles of operation, not at giving you detail about Berkshire's many businesses. For more detail and a continuing update on our progress, you should look to our annual reports. We will be happy to send a copy of our [1997] report to any shareholder requesting it. A great deal of additional information, including our 1977–1996

*Copyright © 1996 By Warren E. Buffett All Rights Reserved. Reprinted by written permission.

annual letters, is available at our Internet site: www.berkshire hathaway.com.

Owner-related Business Principles

At the time of the Blue Chip merger in 1983, I set down 13 owner-related business principles that I thought would help new shareholders understand our managerial approach. As is appropriate for "principles," all 13 remain alive and well today, and they are stated here in italics. A few words have been changed to bring them up-to-date and to each I've added a short commentary.

1. *Although our form is corporate, our attitude is partnership. Charlie Munger and I think of our shareholders as owner-partners, and of ourselves as managing partners. (Because of the size of our shareholdings we are also, for better or worse, controlling partners.) We do not view the company itself as the ultimate owner of our business assets but instead view the company as a conduit through which our shareholders own the assets.*

   Charlie and I hope that you do not think of yourself as merely owning a piece of paper whose price wiggles around daily and that is a candidate for sale when some economic or political event makes you nervous. We hope you instead visualize yourself as a part owner of a business that you expect to stay with indefinitely, much as you might if you owned a farm or apartment house in partnership with members of your family. For our part, we do not view Berkshire shareholders as faceless members of an ever-shifting crowd, but rather as co-venturers who have entrusted their funds to us for what may well turn out to be the remainder of their lives.

   The evidence suggests that most Berkshire shareholders have indeed embraced this long-term partnership concept. The annual percentage turnover in Berkshire's shares is a small fraction of that occurring in the stocks of other major American corporations, even when the shares I own are excluded from the calculation.

In effect, our shareholders behave in respect to their Berkshire stock much as Berkshire itself behaves in respect to companies in which it has an investment. As owners of, say, Coca-Cola or Gillette shares, we think of Berkshire as being a non-managing partner in two extraordinary businesses, in which we measure our success by the long-term progress of the companies rather than by the month-to-month movements of their stocks. In fact, we would not care in the least if several years went by in which there was no trading, or quotation of prices, in the stocks of those companies. If we have good long-term expectations, short-term price changes are meaningless for us except to the extent they offer us an opportunity to increase our ownership at an attractive price.

2. *In line with Berkshire's owner-orientation, most of our directors have a major portion of their net worth invested in the company. We eat our own cooking.*

Charlie's family has 90% or more of its net worth in Berkshire shares; my wife, Susie, and I have more than 99%. In addition, many of my relatives—my sisters and cousins, for example—keep a huge portion of their net worth in Berkshire stock.

Charlie and I feel totally comfortable with this eggs-in-one-basket situation because Berkshire itself owns a wide variety of truly extraordinary businesses. Indeed, we believe that Berkshire is close to being unique in the quality and diversity of the businesses in which it owns either a controlling interest or a minority interest of significance.

Charlie and I cannot promise you results. But we can guarantee that your financial fortunes will move in lockstep with ours for whatever period of time you elect to be our partner. We have no interest in large salaries or options or other means of gaining an "edge" over you. We want to make money only when our partners do and in exactly the same proportion. Moreover, when I do something dumb, I want you to be able to derive some solace from the fact that my financial suffering is proportional to yours.

3. *Our long-term economic goal (subject to some qualifications mentioned later) is to maximize Berkshire's average annual rate of gain in intrinsic business value on a per-share basis. We do not measure the economic significance or performance of Berkshire by its size; we measure by per-share progress. We are certain that the rate of per-share progress will diminish in the future—a greatly enlarged capital base will see to that. But we will be disappointed if our rate does not exceed that of the average large American corporation.*

Since that was written at yearend 1983, our intrinsic value (a topic I'll discuss a bit later) has increased at an annual rate of more than 25%, a pace that has definitely surprised both Charlie and me. Nevertheless the principle just stated remains valid: Operating with large amounts of capital as we do today, we cannot come close to performing as well as we once did with much smaller sums. The best rate of gain in intrinsic value we can even hope for is an average of 15% per annum, and we may well fall far short of that target. Indeed, we think very few large businesses have a chance of compounding intrinsic value at 15% per annum over an extended period of time. So it may be that we will end up meeting our stated goal—being above average—with gains that fall significantly short of 15%.

4. *Our preference would be to reach our goal by directly owning a diversified group of businesses that generate cash and consistently earn above-average returns on capital. Our second choice is to own parts of similar businesses, attained primarily through purchases of marketable common stocks by our insurance subsidiaries. The price and availability of businesses and the need for insurance capital determine any given year's capital allocation.*

As has usually been the case, it is easier today to buy small pieces of outstanding businesses via the stock market than to buy similar businesses in their entirety on a negotiated basis. Nevertheless, we continue to prefer the 100% purchase, and in some years we get lucky: In the last three years, in fact, we made seven acquisitions. Though there will be dry years also, we expect to make a number of acquisitions in the decades to come, and our hope is that they will be large. If these purchases approach the quality of those we have made in the past, Berkshire will be well served.

The challenge for us is to generate ideas as rapidly as we generate cash. In this respect, a depressed stock market is likely to present us with significant advantages. For one thing, it tends to reduce the prices at which entire companies become available for purchase. Second, a depressed market makes it easier for our insurance companies to buy small pieces of wonderful businesses—including additional pieces of businesses we already own—at attractive prices. And third, some of those same wonderful businesses, such as Coca-Cola, are consistent buyers of their own shares, which means that they, and we, gain from the cheaper prices at which they can buy.

Overall, Berkshire and its long-term shareholders benefit from a sinking stock market much as a regular purchaser of food benefits from declining food prices. So when the market plummets—as it will from time to time—neither panic nor mourn. It's good news for Berkshire.

5. *Because of our two-pronged approach to business ownership and because of the limitations of conventional accounting, consolidated reported earnings may reveal relatively little about our true economic performance. Charlie and I, both as owners and managers, virtually ignore such consolidated numbers. However, we will also report to you the earnings of each major business we control, numbers we consider of great importance. These figures, along with other information we will supply about the individual businesses, should generally aid you in making judgments about them.*

To state things simply, we try to give you in the annual report the numbers and other information that really matter. Charlie and I pay a great deal of attention to how well our businesses are doing, and we also work to understand the environment in which each business is operating. For example, is one of our businesses enjoying an industry tailwind or is it facing a headwind? Charlie and I need to know exactly which situation prevails and to adjust our expectations accordingly. We will also pass along our conclusions to you.

Over time, practically all of our businesses have exceeded our expectations. But occasionally we have disappointments, and we will try to be as candid in informing you about those as we are in describing the happier experiences. When we use unconventional measures to chart our progress—for instance, you will be reading in our annual reports about insurance "float"—we will try to explain these concepts and why we regard them as important. In other words, we believe in telling you how we think so that you can evaluate not only Berkshire's businesses but also assess our approach to management and capital allocation.

6. *Accounting consequences do not influence our operating or capital-allocation decisions. When acquisition costs are similar, we much prefer to purchase $2 of earnings that is not reportable by us under standard accounting principles than to purchase $1 of earnings that is reportable. This is precisely the choice that often faces us since entire businesses (whose earnings will be fully reportable) frequently sell for double the pro-rata price of small portions (whose earnings will be largely unreportable). In aggregate and over time, we expect the unreported earnings to be fully reflected in our intrinsic business value through capital gains.*

We attempt to offset the shortcomings of conventional accounting by regularly reporting "look-through" earnings (though, for special and nonrecurring reasons, we occasionally omit them). The look-through numbers include Berkshire's own reported operating earnings, excluding capital gains and purchase-accounting adjustments (an explanation of which occurs later in this message) plus Berkshire's share of the undistributed earnings of our major investees— amounts that are not included in Berkshire's figures under conventional accounting. From these undistributed earnings of our investees we subtract the tax we would have owed had the earnings been paid to us as dividends. We also exclude capital gains, purchase-accounting adjustments and extraordinary charges or credits from the investee numbers.

We have found over time that the undistributed earn-ings of our investees, in aggregate, have been fully as bene-ficial to Berkshire as if they had been distributed to us (and therefore had been included in the earnings we officially report). This pleasant result has occurred because most of our investees are engaged in truly outstanding businesses that can often employ incremental capital to great advan-tage, either by putting it to work in their businesses or by re-purchasing their shares. Obviously, every capital decision that our investees have made has not benefitted us as share-holders, but overall we have garnered far more than a dollar of value for each dollar they have retained. We consequently regard look-through earnings as realistically portraying our yearly gain from operations.

In 1992, our look-through earnings were $604 million, and in that same year we set a goal of raising them by an av-erage of 15% per annum to $1.8 billion in the year 2000. Since that time, however, we have issued additional shares—including a significant number in the 1998 merger with General Re—so that we now need look-through earn-ings of $2.4 billion in 2000 to match the per-share goal we originally were shooting for. This is a target we still hope to hit.

7. *We use debt sparingly and, when we do borrow, we attempt to struc-ture our loans on a long-term fixed-rate basis. We will reject inter-esting opportunities rather than over-leverage our balance sheet. This conservatism has penalized our results but it is the only be-havior that leaves us comfortable, considering our fiduciary obliga-tions to policyholders, lenders and the many equity holders who have committed unusually large portions of their net worth to our care. (As one of the Indianapolis "500" winners said: "To finish first, you must first finish.")*

The financial calculus that Charlie and I employ would never permit our trading a good night's sleep for a shot at a few extra percentage points of return. I've never believed in risking what my family and friends have and need in order to pursue what they don't have and don't need.

Besides, Berkshire has access to two low-cost, non-perilous sources of leverage that allow us to safely own far more assets than our equity capital alone would permit: deferred taxes and "float," the funds of others that our insurance business holds because it receives premiums before needing to pay out losses. Both of these funding sources have grown rapidly and now total about $32 billion.

Better yet, this funding to date has been cost-free. Deferred tax liabilities bear no interest. And as long as we can break even in our insurance underwriting—which we have done, on the average, during our 32 years in the business—the cost of the float developed from that operation is zero. Neither item, of course, is equity; these are real liabilities. But they are liabilities without covenants or due dates attached to them. In effect, they give us the benefit of debt—an ability to have more assets working for us—but saddle us with none of its drawbacks.

Of course, there is no guarantee that we can obtain our float in the future at no cost. But we feel our chances of attaining that goal are as good as those of anyone in the insurance business. Not only have we reached the goal in the past (despite a number of important mistakes by your Chairman), our 1996 acquisition of GEICO materially improved our prospects for getting there in the future.

8. *A managerial "wish list" will not be filled at shareholder expense. We will not diversify by purchasing entire businesses at control prices that ignore long-term economic consequences to our shareholders. We will only do with your money what we would do with our own, weighing fully the values you can obtain by diversifying your own portfolios through direct purchases in the stock market.*

Charlie and I are interested only in acquisitions that we believe will raise the per-share intrinsic value of Berkshire's stock. The size of our paychecks or our offices will never be related to the size of Berkshire's balance sheet.

9. *We feel noble intentions should be checked periodically against results. We test the wisdom of retaining earnings by assessing whether*

retention, over time, delivers shareholders at least $1 of market value for each $1 retained. To date, this test has been met. We will continue to apply it on a five-year rolling basis. As our net worth grows, it is more difficult to use retained earnings wisely.

We continue to pass the test, but the challenges of doing so have grown more difficult. If we reach the point that we can't create extra value by retaining earnings, we will pay them out and let our shareholders deploy the funds.

10. *We will issue common stock only when we receive as much in business value as we give. This rule applies to all forms of issuance—not only mergers or public stock offerings, but stock-for-debt swaps, stock options, and convertible securities as well. We will not sell small portions of your company—and that is what the issuance of shares amounts to—on a basis inconsistent with the value of the entire enterprise.*

When we sold the Class B shares in 1996, we stated that Berkshire stock was not undervalued—and some people found that shocking. That reaction was not well-founded. Shock should have registered instead had we issued shares when our stock was undervalued. Managements that say or imply during a public offering that their stock is undervalued are usually being economical with the truth or uneconomical with their existing shareholders' money: Owners unfairly lose if their managers deliberately sell assets for 80¢; that in fact are worth $1. We didn't commit that kind of crime in our offering of Class B shares and we never will. (We did not, however, say at the time of the sale that our stock was overvalued, though many media have reported that we did.)

11. *You should be fully aware of one attitude Charlie and I share that hurts our financial performance: Regardless of price, we have no interest at all in selling any good businesses that Berkshire owns. We are also very reluctant to sell sub-par businesses as long as we expect them to generate at least some cash and as long as we feel good about their managers and labor relations. We hope not to repeat the capital-allocation mistakes that led us into such sub-par businesses.*

And we react with great caution to suggestions that our poor businesses can be restored to satisfactory profitability by major capital expenditures. (The projections will be dazzling and the advocates sincere, but, in the end, major additional investment in a terrible industry usually is about as rewarding as struggling in quicksand.) Nevertheless, gin rummy managerial behavior (discard your least promising business at each turn) is not our style. We would rather have our overall results penalized a bit than engage in that kind of behavior.

We continue to avoid gin rummy behavior. True, we closed our textile business in the mid-1980's after 20 years of struggling with it, but only because we felt it was doomed to run never-ending operating losses. We have not, however, given thought to selling operations that would command very fancy prices nor have we dumped our laggards, though we focus hard on curing the problems that cause them to lag.

12. *We will be candid in our reporting to you, emphasizing the pluses and minuses important in appraising business value. Our guideline is to tell you the business facts that we would want to know if our positions were reversed. We owe you no less. Moreover, as a company with a major communications business, it would be inexcusable for us to apply lesser standards of accuracy, balance and incisiveness when reporting on ourselves than we would expect our news people to apply when reporting on others. We also believe candor benefits us as managers: The CEO who misleads others in public may eventually mislead himself in private.*

At Berkshire you will find no "big bath" accounting maneuvers or restructurings nor any "smoothing" of quarterly or annual results. We will always tell you how many strokes we have taken on each hole and never play around with the scorecard. When the numbers are a very rough "guesstimate," as they necessarily must be in insurance reserving, we will try to be both consistent and conservative in our approach.

We will be communicating with you in several ways. Through the annual report, I try to give all shareholders as much value-defining information as can be conveyed in a document kept to reasonable length. We also try to convey a liberal quantity of condensed but important information in our quarterly reports, though I don't write those (one recital a year is enough). Still another important occasion for communication is our Annual Meeting, at which Charlie and I are delighted to spend five hours or more answering questions about Berkshire. But there is one way we can't communicate: on a one-on-one basis. That isn't feasible given Berkshire's many thousands of owners.

In all of our communications, we try to make sure that no single shareholder gets an edge: We do not follow the usual practice of giving earnings "guidance" or other information of value to analysts or large shareholders. Our goal is to have all of our owners updated at the same time.

13. *Despite our policy of candor, we will discuss our activities in marketable securities only to the extent legally required. Good investment ideas are rare, valuable and subject to competitive appropriation just as good product or business acquisition ideas are. Therefore we normally will not talk about our investment ideas. This ban extends even to securities we have sold (because we may purchase them again) and to stocks we are incorrectly rumored to be buying. If we deny those reports but say "no comment" on other occasions, the no-comments become confirmation.*

Though we continue to be unwilling to talk about specific stocks, we freely discuss our business and investment philosophy. I benefitted enormously from the intellectual generosity of Ben Graham, the greatest teacher in the history of finance, and I believe it appropriate to pass along what I learned from him, even if that creates new and able investment competitors for Berkshire just as Ben's teachings did for him.

An Added Principle

To the extent possible, we would like each Berkshire shareholder to record a gain or loss in market value during his period of ownership that is proportional to the gain or loss in per-share intrinsic value recorded by the company during that holding period. For this to come about, the relationship between the intrinsic value and the market price of a Berkshire share would need to remain constant, and by our preferences at 1-to-1. As that implies, we would rather see Berkshire's stock price at a fair level than a high level. Obviously, Charlie and I can't control Berkshire's price. But by our policies and communications, we can encourage informed, rational behavior by owners that, in turn, will tend to produce a stock price that is also rational. Our it's-as-bad-to-be-over-valued-as-to-be-undervalued approach may disappoint some shareholders. We believe, however, that it affords Berkshire the best prospect of attracting long-term investors who seek to profit from the progress of the company rather than from the investment mistakes of their partners.

Intrinsic Value

Now let's focus on two terms that I mentioned earlier and that you will encounter in future annual reports. Let's start with intrinsic value, an all-important concept that offers the only logical approach to evaluating the relative attractiveness of investments and businesses. Intrinsic value can be defined simply: It is the discounted value of the cash that can be taken out of a business during its remaining life.

The calculation of intrinsic value, though, is not so simple. As our definition suggests, intrinsic value is an estimate rather than a precise figure, and it is additionally an estimate that must be changed if interest rates move or forecasts of future cash flows are revised. Two people looking at the same set of facts, moreover—and this would apply even to Charlie and me—will almost inevitably come up with at least slightly different intrinsic value figures. That is one reason we never give you our estimates of intrinsic value. What our annual reports do supply, though, are the facts that we ourselves use to calculate this value.

Meanwhile, we regularly report our per-share book value, an easily calculable number, though one of limited use. The limitations do not arise from our holdings of marketable securities, which are carried on our books at their current prices. Rather the inadequacies of book value have to do with the companies we control, whose values as stated on our books may be far different from their intrinsic values.

The disparity can go in either direction. For example, in 1964 we could state with certitude that Berkshire's per-share book value was $19.46. However, that figure considerably overstated the company's intrinsic value, since all of the company's resources were tied up in a sub-profitable textile business. Our textile assets had neither going—concern nor liquidation values equal to their carrying values. Today, however, Berkshire's situation is reversed: Now, our book value far understates Berkshire's intrinsic value, a point true because many of the businesses we control are worth much more than their carrying value.

Inadequate though they are in telling the story, we give you Berkshire's book-value figures because they today serve as a rough, albeit significantly understated, tracking measure for Berkshire's intrinsic value. In other words, the percentage change in book value in any given year is likely to be reasonably close to that year's change in intrinsic value.

You can gain some insight into the differences between book value and intrinsic value by looking at one form of investment, a college education. Think of the education's cost as its "book value." If this cost is to be accurate, it should include the earnings that were foregone by the student because he chose college rather than a job.

For this exercise, we will ignore the important non-economic benefits of an education and focus strictly on its economic value. First, we must estimate the earnings that the graduate will receive over his lifetime and subtract from that figure an estimate of what he would have earned had he lacked his education. That gives us an excess earnings figure, which must then be discounted, at an appropriate interest rate, back to graduation day. The dollar result equals the intrinsic economic value of the education.

Some graduates will find that the book value of their education exceeds its intrinsic value, which means that whoever paid for the education didn't get his money's worth. In other cases, the intrinsic value of an education will far exceed its book value, a result that proves capital was wisely deployed. In all cases, what is clear is that book value is meaningless as an indicator of intrinsic value.

Purchase-accounting Adjustments

Next: spinach time. I know that a discussion of accounting technicalities turns off many readers, so let me assure you that a full and happy life can still be yours if you decide to skip this section.

Our 1996 acquisition of GEICO, however, means that purchase-accounting adjustments of about $40 million are charged against our annual earnings as recorded under generally accepted accounting principles (GAAP). Our General Re acquisition will produce an annual charge many times this number, but we don't have final figures at this time. The magnitude of these changes makes them a subject of importance to Berkshire. In our annual reports, therefore, we will sometimes talk of earnings that we will describe as "before purchase-accounting adjustments." The discussion that follows will tell you why we think earnings of that description have far more economic meaning than the earnings produced by GAAP.

When Berkshire buys a business for a premium over the GAAP net worth of the acquiree—as will usually be the case, since most companies we'd want to buy don't come at a discount—that premium has to be entered on the asset side of our balance sheet. There are loads of rules about just how a company should record the premium. But to simplify this discussion, we will focus on "Goodwill," the asset item to which almost all of Berkshire's acquisition premiums have been allocated. For example, when we acquired in 1996 the half of GEICO we didn't previously own, we recorded goodwill of about $1.6 billion.

GAAP requires goodwill to be amortized—that is, written off—over a period no longer than 40 years. Therefore, to extinguish our $1.6 billion in GEICO goodwill, we will take annual charges of about $40 million until 2036. This amount is not deductible for tax purposes, so it reduces both our pre-tax and after-tax earnings by $40 million.

In an accounting sense, consequently, our GEICO goodwill will disappear gradually in even-sized bites. But the one thing I

can guarantee you is that the economic goodwill we have purchased at GEICO will not decline in the same measured way. In
fact, my best guess is that the economic goodwill assignable to
GEICO has dramatically increased since our purchase and will
likely continue to increase—quite probably in a very substantial
way.

I made a similar statement in our 1983 Annual Report about
the goodwill attributed to See's Candy, when I used that company as an example in a discussion of goodwill accounting. At
that time, our balance sheet carried about $36 million of See's
goodwill. We have since been charging about $1 million against
earnings every year in order to amortize the asset, and the See's
goodwill on our balance sheet is now down to about $21 million.
In other words, from an accounting standpoint, See's is now pre-
sented as having lost a good deal of goodwill since 1983.

The economic facts could not be more different. In 1983,
See's earned about $27 million pre-tax on $11 million of net operating assets; in 1997 it earned $59 million on $5 million of net
operating assets. Clearly See's economic goodwill has increased
dramatically during the interval rather than decreased. Just as
clearly, See's is worth many hundreds of millions of dollars more
than its stated value on our books.

We could, of course, be wrong, but we expect that GEICO's
gradual loss of accounting value will continue to be paired with
major increases in its economic value. Certainly that has been
the pattern at most of our subsidiaries, not just See's. That is why
we regularly present our operating earnings in a way that allows
you to ignore all purchase-accounting adjustments.

Before leaving this subject, we should issue an important
warning: Investors are often led astray by CEOs and Wall Street
analysts who equate depreciation charges with the amortization
charges we have just discussed. In no way are the two the same:
With rare exceptions, depreciation is an economic cost every bit
as real as wages, materials, or taxes. Certainly that is true at
Berkshire and at virtually all the other businesses we have stud-
ied. Furthermore, we do not think so-called EBITDA (earnings
before interest, taxes, depreciation and amortization) is a meaningful measure of performance. Managements that dismiss the

importance of depreciation—and emphasize "cash flow" or EBITDA—are apt to make faulty decisions, and you should keep that in mind as you make your own investment decisions.

The Managing of Berkshire

I think it's appropriate that I conclude with a discussion of Berkshire's management, today and in the future. As our first owner-related principle tells you, Charlie and I are the managing partners of Berkshire. But we subcontract all of the heavy lifting in this business to the managers of our subsidiaries. In fact, we delegate almost to the point of abdication: Though Berkshire has about 45,000 employees, only 12 of these are at headquarters.

Charlie and I mainly attend to capital allocation and the care and feeding of our key managers. Most of these managers are happiest when they are left alone to run their businesses, and that is customarily just how we leave them. That puts them in charge of all operating decisions and of dispatching the excess cash they generate to headquarters. By sending it to us, they don't get diverted by the various enticements that would come their way were they responsible for deploying the cash their businesses throw off. Furthermore, Charlie and I are exposed to a much wider range of possibilities for investing these funds than any of our managers could find in his or her own industry.

Most of our managers are independently wealthy, and it's therefore up to us to create a climate that encourages them to choose working with Berkshire over golfing or fishing. This leaves us needing to treat them fairly and in the manner that we would wish to be treated if our positions were reversed.

As for the allocation of capital, that's an activity both Charlie and I enjoy and in which we have acquired some useful experience. In a general sense, grey hair doesn't hurt on this playing field: You don't need good hand-eye coordination or well-toned muscles to push money around (thank heavens). As long as our minds continue to function effectively, Charlie and I can keep on doing our jobs pretty much as we have in the past.

On my death, Berkshire's ownership picture will change but not in a disruptive way: First, only about 1% of my stock will have to be sold to take care of bequests and taxes; second, the balance of my stock will go to my wife, Susan, if she survives me, or to a family foundation if she doesn't. In either event, Berkshire will possess a controlling shareholder guided by the same philosophy and objectives that now set our course.

At that juncture, the Buffett family will not be involved in managing the business, only in picking and overseeing the managers who do. Just who those managers will be, of course, depends on the date of my death. But I can anticipate what the management structure will be: Essentially my job will be split into two parts, with one executive becoming responsible for investments and another for operations. If the acquisition of new businesses is in prospect, the two will cooperate in making the decisions needed. Both executives will report to a board of directors who will be responsive to the controlling shareholder, whose interests will in turn be aligned with yours.

Were we to need the management structure I have just described on an immediate basis, my family and a few key individuals know who I would pick to fill both posts. Both currently work for Berkshire and are people in whom I have total confidence.

I will continue to keep my family posted on the succession issue. Since Berkshire stock will make up virtually my entire estate and will account for a similar portion of the assets of either my wife or the foundation for a considerable period after my death, you can be sure that I have thought through the succession question carefully. You can be equally sure that the principles we have employed to date in running Berkshire will continue to guide the managers who succeed me.

Lest we end on a morbid note, I also want to assure you that I have never felt better. I love running Berkshire, and if enjoying life promotes longevity, Methuselah's record is in jeopardy.

Warren E. Buffett
Chairman

Appendix IX

Business Activities

B erkshire Hathaway Inc. is a holding company owning subsidiaries engaged in a number of diverse business activities. The most important of these is the property and casualty insurance business conducted on both a direct and reinsurance basis through a number of subsidiaries. Included in this group of subsidiaries is GEICO Corporation, the sixth largest auto insurer in the United States and General Re Corporation, one of the four largest reinsurers in the world.

Investment portfolios of insurance subsidiaries include meaningful equity ownership percentages of other publicly traded companies. Investments in excess of 5 percent of the investees outstanding capital stock at the end of 1998 include approximately 11 percent of the outstanding capital stock of American Express Company, approximately 8 percent of the capital stock of The Coca-Cola Company, approximately 9 percent of the capital stock of Federal HomeLoan Mortgage Corporation ("Freddie Mac"), approximately 8½ percent of the capital stock of The Gillette Company, and approximately 17 percent of the capital stock of The Washington Post Company. Much information about these publicly-owned companies is available, including information released from time to time by the companies themselves.

Other business activities conducted by non-insurance subsidiaries include publication of a daily and Sunday newspaper in Western New York (Buffalo News), manufacture and sale of boxed chocolates and other confectionery products (See's

Candies), diversified manufacturing and distribution (managed by Scott Fetzer and whose principal products are sold under the Kirby and Campbell Hausfeld brand names), retailing of home furnishings (Nebraska Furniture Mart, R.C. Willey Home Furnishings, Star Furniture Company, and Jordan's Furniture), manufacture, import and distribution of footwear (H.H. Brown Shoe Company, Lowell Shoe, Inc., Dexter Shoe Company, and Justin Brand Boots), retailing of fine jewelry (Borsheim's, Helzberg's Diamond Shops, and Ben Bridge), training to operators of aircraft and ships throughout the world (FlightSafety International), providing fractional ownership programs for general aviation aircraft (Executive Jet), and licensing and servicing a system of approximately 5,900 Dairy Queen stores.

Operating decisions for the various Berkshire businesses are made by managers of the business units. Investment decisions and all their capital allocation decisions are made for Berkshire and its subsidiaries by Warren E. Buffett, in consultation with Charles T. Munger. Mr. Buffett is Chairman and Mr. Munger is Vice Chairman of Berkshire's Board of Directors.

Appendix X

Common Stock

General

The Company has two classes of common stock designated Class A Common Stock [NYSE: BRK.A] and Class B Common Stock [NYSE: BRK.B]. Each share of Class A Common Stock is convertible, at the option of the holder, into 30 shares of Class B Common Stock. Shares of Class B Common Stock are not convertible into shares of Class A Common Stock.

Stock Transfer Agent

BankBoston, N.A. c/o Boston EquiServe, P.O. Box 8040, Boston, MA 02266-8040 serves as Transfer Agent and Registrar for the Company's common stock. Correspondence may be directed to Investor Relations, Mail Stop 45-02-64. Certificates for re-issue or transfer should be directed to the Transfer Processing Section, Mail Stop 45-01-05. Notices for conversion and underlying stock certificates should be directed to Corporate Reorganization, Mail Stop 45-02-53. Phone inquiries should be directed to Investor Relations—(781) 575-3100.

Shareholders of record wishing to convert Class A Common Stock into Class B Common Stock should contact BankBoston to obtain a "form of conversion notice" and instructions for converting their shares. Shareholders may call BankBoston between 9:00 a.m. and 6:00 p.m. Eastern Time to request a "form of conversion notice."

Alternatively, shareholders may notify BankBoston in writing. Along with the underlying stock certificate, shareholders should provide BankBoston with specific written instructions regarding the number of shares to be converted and the manner in which the Class B shares are to be registered. We recommend that you use certified or registered mail when delivering the stock certificates and written instructions.

If Class A shares are held in "street name", shareholders wishing to convert all or a portion of their holding should contact their broker or bank nominee. It will be necessary for the nominee to make the request for conversion.

Shareholders

The Company had approximately 9,300 record holders of its Class A Common Stock and 13,400 record holders of its Class B Common Stock at March 5, 1999. Record owners included nominees holding at least 385,000 shares of Class A Common Stock and 4,850,000 shares of Class B Common Stock on behalf of beneficial-but-not-of-record owners.

Price Range of Common Stock

The Company's Class A and Class B Common Stock are listed for trading on the New York Stock Exchange, trading symbol: BRK.A and BRK.B. The following figure sets forth the high and low sales prices per share, as reported on the New York Stock Exchange Composite List during the periods indicated:

	1999				1998			
	Class A		*Class B*		*Class A*		*Class B*	
Qtr	*High*	*Low*	*High*	*Low*	*High*	*Low*	*High*	*Low*
1	$81,100	$61,900	$2,713	$2,048	$69,500	$45,700	$2,324	$1,526
2	78,600	68,300	2,540	2,211	84,000	65,800	2,795	2,184
3	73,000	54,600	2,333	1,802	78,500	57,000	2,622	1,893
4	66,900	52,000	2,219	1,700½	71,000	57,700	2,396	1,916

Dividends

Berkshire has not declared a cash dividend since 1967.

Appendix XI

Shareholder-designated Contributions

The Company has conducted this program of corporate giving during each of the past eighteen years. On October 14, 1981, the Chairman sent to the shareholders a letter* explaining the program. Portions of that letter follow:

"On September 30, 1981 Berkshire received a tax ruling from the U.S. Treasury Department that, in most years, should produce a significant benefit for charities of your choice."

"Each Berkshire shareholder—on a basis proportional to the number of shares of Berkshire that he owns—will be able to designate recipients of charitable contributions by our company. You'll name the charity; Berkshire will write the check. The ruling states that there will be no personal tax consequences to our shareholders from making such designations.

"Thus, our approximately 1500 owners now can exercise a perquisite that, although routinely exercised by the owners in closely-held businesses, is almost exclusively exercised by the managers in more widely-held businesses.

"In a widely-held corporation the executives ordinarily arrange all charitable donations, with no input at all from shareholders, in two main categories:

(1) *Donations considered to benefit the corporation directly in an amount roughly commensurate with the cost of the donation; and*

(2) *Donations considered to benefit the corporation indirectly through hard-to-measure, long-delayed feedback effects of various kinds.*

"I and other Berkshire executives have arranged in the past, as we will arrange in the future, all charitable donations in the first category. However, the aggregate level of giving in such category has been quite low, and very likely will remain quite low, because not many gifts can be shown to produce roughly commensurate direct benefits to Berkshire.

"In the second category, Berkshire's charitable gifts have been virtually nil, because I am not comfortable with ordinary corporate practice and had no better practice to substitute. What bothers me about ordinary corporate practice is the way gifts tend to be made based more on who does the asking and how corporate peers are responding than on an objective evaluation of the donee's activities. Conventionality often overpowers rationality.

"A common result is the use of the stockholder's money to implement the charitable inclinations of the corporate manager, who usually is heavily influenced by specific social pressures on him. Frequently there is an added incongruity; many corporate managers deplore governmental allocation of the taxpayer's dollar but embrace enthusiastically their own allocation of the shareholder's dollar.

"For Berkshire, a different model seems appropriate. Just as I wouldn't want you to implement your personal judgments by writing checks on my bank account for charities of your choice, I feel it inappropriate to write checks on your corporate "bank account" for charities of my choice. Your charitable preferences are as good as mine and, for both you and me, funds available to foster charitable interests in a tax-deductible manner reside largely at the corporate level rather than in our own hands.

"Under such circumstances, I believe Berkshire should imitate more closely-held companies, not larger public companies. If you and I each own 50% of a corporation, our charitable decision making would be simple. Charities very directly related to the operations of the business would have first claim on our available charitable funds. Any balance available after the "operations-related" contributions would be divided among various charitable interests of the two of us, on a basis roughly proportional to our ownership interest. If the manager of our company had some suggestions, we would listen carefully—but the final decision would be ours. Despite our corporate form, in this aspect of the business we probably would behave as if we were a partnership.

"Wherever feasible, I believe in maintaining such a partnership frame of mind, even though we operate through a large, fairly widely-held corporation. Our Treasury ruling will allow such partnership-like behavior in this area.

"I am pleased that Berkshire donations can become owner-directed. It is ironic, but understandable, that a large and growing number of major corporations have charitable policies pursuant to which they will match gifts made by their employees (and—brace yourself for this one—many even match gifts made by directors) but none, to my knowledge, has a plan matching charitable gifts by owners. I say "understandable" because much of the stock of many large corporations is owned on a "revolving door" basis by institutions that have short-term investment horizons, and that lack a long-term owner's perspective.

"Our own shareholders are a different breed. As I mentioned in the 1979 annual report, at the end of each year more than 98% of our shares are owned by people who were shareholders at the beginning of the year. This long-term commitment to the business reflects an owner mentality which, as your manager, I intend to acknowledge in all feasible ways. The designated contributions policy is an example of that intent."

The history of contributions made pursuant to this program since its inception follows:

Year	Percent of Specified Amount per share	Eligible* Shares Participating	Amount Contributed	No. of Charities
1981	$2	95.6%	$ 1,783,655	675
1982	$1	95.8%	$ 890,948	704
1983	$3	96.4%	$ 3,066,501	1,353
1984	$3	97.2%	$ 3,179,049	1,519
1985	$4	96.8%	$ 4,006,260	1,724
1986	$4	97.1%	$ 3,996,820	1,934
1987	$5	97.2%	$ 4,937,574	2,050
1988	$5	97.4%	$ 4,965,665	2,319
1989	$6	96.9%	$ 5,867,254	2,550
1990	$6	97.3%	$ 5,823,672	2,600
1991	$7	97.7%	$ 6,772,024	2,630
1992	$8	97.0%	$ 7,634,784	2,810
1993	$10	97.3%	$ 9,448,370	3,110
1994	$11	95.7%	$10,419,497	3,330
1995	$12	96.3%	$11,558,616	3,600
1996	$14	97.2%	$13,309,044	3,910
1997	$16	97.7%	$15,424,480	3,830
1998	$18	97.5%	$16,931,538	3,880
1999	$18	97.3%	$17,174,158	3,850

*Shares registered in street name are not eligible to participate.

In addition to the shareholder-designated contributions summarized above, Berkshire and its subsidiaries have made certain contributions pursuant to local level decisions of operating managers of the businesses.

The program may not be conducted in the occasional year, if any, when the contributions would produce substandard or no tax deductions. In other years Berkshire expects to inform shareholders of the amount per share that may be designated, and a reply form will accompany the notice allowing shareholders to respond with their designations. If the program is conducted in 2001, the notice will be mailed on or about September 15 to Class A shareholders of record reflected in our Registrar's records as of the close of business August 31, 2001, and shareholders will be given until November 15 to respond.

Shareholders should note the fact that Class A shares held in street name are not eligible to participate in the program. To qualify, shares must be registered with our Registrar on August 31 in the owner's individual name(s) or the name of an owning trust, corporation, partnership or estate, as applicable. Also, shareholders should note that Class B shares are not eligible to participate in the program.

Appendix XII

Contributions Program Commonly Asked Questions

Eligibility Requirements of Shareholders

Q. Are both Class A and Class B shareholders eligible to participate?

A. Owners of Class A shares on August 31, 2001 may be eligible, depending on how the shares are registered or held. To be eligible, your Class A shares must be held by you in certificate form on August 31. Class A shares held in street name on that date are not eligible. Class B shares are ineligible regardless of how they are registered or held.

Q. What does it mean when shares are "held in street name" and why is this significant?

A. There are basically two ways that your ownership may be represented. Shares may be held in the form of a certificate issued by Berkshire's stock transfer agent and registered in the name of the owning individual, corporation, partnership, or trust. Shares may also be held by an intermediary bank or broker, who in turn holds the shares for your direct benefit. The latter category is referred to as shares held in "street name". The bank or broker is responsible for maintaining records of beneficial ownership and Berkshire does not have access to such records. Since Berkshire does not know the identity of beneficial owners of Class A shares held in street name, all such shares are ineligible.

Q. I owned Class A shares that were in street name on August 31 in addition to those held directly in my name. May I make a designation with respect to shares held in street name?

A. No. The shares registered in street name are not eligible to participate; only the shares registered directly in your name are eligible.

Q. Can Class A shares held in an Individual Retirement Account be eligible to participate?

A. Class A shares in IRA's that are held in street name are ineligible. Due to income tax restrictions on IRA's, you will need to make special arrangements with your bank/broker to be the custodian of your Class A shares, which would be reissued into certificate form. If properly registered in certificate form, your Class A shares would be eligible to participate. You should contact your bank/broker and Berkshire's stock transfer agent for exact instructions on how this may be accomplished.

Eligibility Requirements of Charities

Q. Is it possible for me to designate more than three charities to receive a part of the total amount that I am entitled to designate?

A. You may designate no more than three qualified charities to receive the "entitlement" amount shown on the designation form. The number of charities is also limited to your number of Class A shares if less than three.

Q. Will the Company make a contribution pursuant to my designation to any cause I deem worthy, even to a charity not qualified by the IRS?

A. We will make contributions only to organizations qualified to receive tax deductible donations. We refer to Publication No. 78 of the U.S. Treasury Department to determine whether an organization is a qualified charity.

Q. May I nominate a charity to receive a donation from Berkshire in satisfaction of my personal "pledge" to that charity?

A. No. Satisfaction of your personal pledge with a donation from this program is deemed an economic benefit to you, which is prohibited. The form that you sign and return to Berkshire contains a warranty that you do not receive any economic benefit from the donation.

Deadline for Submitting Charitable Contribution Forms

Q. How will Berkshire determine timely receipt of my contribution form?

A. We will mail a charitable nomination form to you on or about September 15. We must physically receive your completed form by the November 15 deadline to be timely. We do not base timely receipt on the post mark date of your response.

Q. Will Berkshire accept my form by fax?

A. Due to the large volume of forms processed and limited fax resources, we will not accept completed forms via fax.

Tax Consequences

Q. Are there any tax consequences to me as a result of this program?

A. The amounts that you designate are neither income to you nor are you entitled to a tax deduction on your income tax return. This result is predicated upon your not receiving any personal economic benefit from the donation. The contribution form that you return to Berkshire contains your warranty to that effect. Berkshire or a Berkshire subsidiary is solely entitled to the tax deductions arising from the contribution.

Other Matters

Q. Will the Company contact me if it has questions about my reply form?

A. Probably not. The number of shareholders has increased beyond the point where that is practical. If the charity has not been listed in Publication No. 78, and it is not otherwise obvious to us that the designee is an IRS qualified charity, the Company may not act on the designation. Berkshire may at its discretion disregard all or part of your designation form if it believes any of the program rules are violated.

Q. Will the charity know that it received the contribution because of my designation?

A. Unless you request anonymity, a voucher will be attached to the contribution check when it is sent, showing your name and address exactly as it appears in the reply form enclosed. (Changes to your name or address will not be made for purposes of this program.)

Q. When should I call or write to the Company to inform it that my designated contribution has not been received by the charity?

A. Please write, but not until after March 31. Only limited possibilities for Company investigation exist before that time because canceled contribution checks for the 2001 program will likely not have been returned before early February.

Appendix XIII

Acquisition Criteria

We are eager to hear from principals or their representatives about businesses that meet all of the following criteria:

(1) Large purchases (at least $50 million of before-tax earnings),

(2) Demonstrated consistent earning power (future projections are of no interest to us, nor are "turnaround" situations),

(3) Businesses earning good returns on equity while employing little or no debt,

(4) Management in place (we can't supply it),

(5) Simple businesses (if there's lots of technology, we won't understand it),

(6) An offering price (we don't want to waste our time or that of the seller by talking, even preliminarily, about a transaction when price is unknown).

The larger the company, the greater will be our interest: We would like to make an acquisition in the $5–20 billion range. We are not interested, however, in receiving suggestions about purchases we might make in the general stock market.

We will not engage in unfriendly takeovers. We can promise complete confidentiality and a very fast answer—customarily within five minutes—as to whether we're interested. We prefer to buy for cash, but will consider issuing stock when we receive as much in intrinsic business value as we give.

Charlie and I frequently get approached about acquisitions that don't come close to meeting our tests: We've found that if you advertise an interest in buying collies, a lot of people will call hoping to sell you their cocker spaniels. A line from a country song expresses our feeling about new ventures, turnarounds, or auction-like sales: "When the phone don't ring, you'll know it's me."

Appendix XIV

Other Information about Berkshire

Letters from Annual Reports (1977 through 1999), quarterly reports, press releases and other information about Berkshire may be obtained on the Internet at www.berkshirehathaway .com. In addition, this site includes links to the home pages of many Berkshire subsidiaries. A three volume bound set of compilations of letters (1977 through 1999) is available upon written request accompanied by a payment of $35.00 to cover production, postage and handling costs. Requests should be submitted to the Company at 3555 Farnam St., Suite 1440, Omaha, NE 68131.

Appendix XV

Answers to #45, Buy 1 Stock Get 100 Companies (page 61)

A. American Express
B. Borsheim's
C. Coke
D. Dexter
E. Executive Jet
F. Flight Safety
G. GEICO/Gillette
H. Helzberg Diamond Shops
I. International Dairy Queen
J. Jordan's Furniture
K. Kirby
L. Lowell Shoes
M. Meriam (pressure and flow measurement devices)
N. Nebraska Furniture Mart
O. Omaha
P. Precision Steel
Q. Quikut Knives
R. R.C. Willey Home Furnishings
S. See's Candies
T. The Washington Post

U. United States Liability Insurance Group
V. Value
W. World Book Encyclopedias
X. X-factor
Y. Yellow Brkers
Z. Zuckerberg's Uniforms (Indianapolis)

Appendix XVI

Berkshire (Class A) Year-end Closing Prices

	'A' share		'A' share	'B' share
1967	$20.50	1984	1,275	
1968	36	1985	2,430	
1969	43	1986	2,820	
1970	41	1987	2,950	
1971	74	1988	4,700	
1972	80	1989	8,675	
1973	78	1990	6,675	
1974	40	1991	9,050	
1975	41	1992	11,750	
1976	94	1993	16,325	
1977	138	1994	20,400	
1978	158	1995	32,100	
1979	320	1996	34,100	1,112
1980	425	1997	46,000	1,534
1981	560	1998	70,000	2,350
1982	775	1999	56,100	1,830
1983	1,310	2000	71,000	2,354

Appendix XVII

A Very Personal Experience

One of the most amazing things about Berkshire is how very personal it is. Just about every shareholder has a story to tell regarding their ownership. From all walks of life and all different backgrounds from all parts of the United States and the world make this Berkshire family diverse and unique.

What this reason seeks (the first in a series of a hundred more) is a collection of various stories that in their collective will be a powerful message, for: the shareholder next door, the midlevel manager, the stay at home mom, the student, the retiree, the unsophisticated as well as the sophisticated. This reason is seeking all types from different backgrounds to point out that the Berkshire village is diverse, alive and well, and surprisingly, a lot like you.

Maybe you found Berkshire to preserve family wealth and to pass on to your children. Maybe Berkshire has funded your retirement, your children's education, a vacation home, a new business, medical expenses, a favorite charity or a trip around the world. Whatever your story my request is to hear from the Berkshire family and to include your experience in an updated version or Berkshire 201, the sequel.

Commonly Berkshire shareholders are thought to be high-powered executives and financial whiz moguls. Billionaires and millionaires out of touch with the common people. Who else could afford such a high priced stock. Jet setters in search of conspicuous consumption.

When in fact reality is quite the contrary. If you've attended an annual meeting you know the Berkshire clan to be friendly, down home, neighborly, as well as diverse. Berkshire is very much about family. Berkshire is very personal.

I am thinking of the California psychologist who 15 years ago invested $40,000 of his retirement funds in Berkshire. He did so after getting a recommendation from his mother's financial advisor and after reading everything he could about Mr. Buffett and the company. His modest Berkshire retirement fund has grown into several million dollars and he writes that not a day goes by where he doesn't think about Berkshire.

Or the very personal story of the housewife from Omaha who doesn't even own Berkshire but uses it to expand her financial education. Fortunately for her, she can attend the annual meeting without much sacrifice. Most importantly she has taken the time to get to know Berkshire and it has provided her with the best learning experience. It's been a free investment education. And she has met some wonderful shareholders from all over the country and one as far away as Australia.

How about the new investor in Atlanta that recently made her first investment in Berkshire. She wrote to say that Berkshire has taught her how to make the right investments. Berkshire is her investment road map.

Even an investment professional in New York who has been a long term owner of Berkshire writes to say that Berkshire is his method to create and preserve his family's wealth, fund his children's education, and provide for his retirement. He hopes Berkshire will always be part of his family's investment portfolio.

One relatively new investor made her first trip to Omaha to meet the man who was in charge of her largest investment and was amazed at how much energy Mr. Buffett had. Some things, like her investment portfolio and manager need to be judged in person. She was also struck by how family oriented the meeting was with many first wives in attendance.

What all of these people have in common is the search for the financial truth and to hire the best money management team available. They willingly make their pilgrimage to the annual meeting to learn, to inquire, to better understand, to confirm their investment beliefs, to show their appreciation, to network, to shop at the company stores and to buy the company's products and services.

Many traders, financial professionals and do it yourselfers are drawn to Omaha to emulate and justify their financial moves. They spend a great deal of energy trying to read into every word and comment by Mr. Buffett; picking out that which confirms their beliefs and ignoring the rest. For this group Berkshire hasn't been very personal.

Have you ever-noticed how very personal business ownership is? Have you been impressed with an entrepreneur's willingness to put it all on the line, to risk it like there's no tomorrow?

Business ownership is so personal that owners will work harder than they have ever worked in their lives for sometimes no compensation. Business ownership is so personal that the proprietor will put his or her name on the business. When you complain about a business, it's the owner who is generally most interested in your complaint.

Business owners take their creation so personal that they will continue a business well past its useful life. It's their baby. And every baby is personal. Maybe this is why only 30 percent of all businesses survive past the original owner's management.

Smith Supply Co. and Johnson Manufacturing Inc. are a direct reflection of the founder, creator, care giver, nurturer, life supporter, visionary, leader, energizer, and chief cook and bottle washer. Their name is on the business, the letterhead, the building and the delivery trucks. Their name is how the phone is answered. Their employees are a reflection of them; hired in their image. For Ms. Smith and Mr. Johnson, their ownership is very personal, and it should be.

It should also be no surprise that there is a very close relationship between the personal experience that an owner of a business has with a shareholder of Berkshire. Both should be a very personal experience. To be a business owner, or at least to think like one, is to be able to best understand Berkshire.

There are Berkshire shareholders and Berkshire owner fanatics. Mostly fanatics and that's a good thing. Remember the fellow on the company meeting video Robert Soener (and also mentioned in *Forbes* magazine Oct 12, 1998 p. 115) who said, "There are three things in my life: God, Warren Buffett and my wife, and I'm not sure about the order of the first two."

And Berkshire owner/partners enjoy the fact that the majority of operating managers are owners and are worth more that $100 million dollars. So Berkshire is very personal to the operating managers/employees as well.

Mr. Buffett takes his ownership in Berkshire very personal and he is mindful that the best shareholders are ones that think of the business like he does in a very personal way. He has gone to extraordinary lengths to attract and keep managers and owners who believe and act like they are partners in the business. His company is the only one to create 14 OWNER-related principles outlined in the OWNER'S manual and an OWNER designated contribution program.

Maybe you have a Berkshire story to tell. If so, please write about your Berkshire experience and e-mail me at robertpmiles@yahoo.com

or mail to:

4532 W. Kennedy Blvd. #275
Tampa, FL 33609-2042

Communication is always best when it's personal. Some of you who have read my first series, Berkshire 101 know how very personal Berkshire is to me. I wrote with sincerity and candor. I had the courage to admit my mistakes. It turned out to be a very cathartic experience. You may find it to be just as liberating.

So make your story as personal as you are comfortable. The best ones will become part of an updated edition.

So the first reason is really an interactive reason from the collective Berkshire community. Defined by you. Told by you. In your own words. No rules. No word length minimum or maximum. Just the way you want it. Hope you're up for the challenge. Entertain us with your very personal Berkshire story.

About the Author

Robert Miles is an entrepreneur, small businessman, and life-long student of investing. Born and raised in Detroit, he is a graduate of The University of Michigan with a bachelor's degree in business administration.

Mr. Miles' writing perspective is as a decade trader in an era of day trading. His approach and passionate statements are from a private investor, business owner and shareholder.

Originally, Mr. Miles wrote this book in just 3½ months on the Internet in full view of investors, shareholders, the financial industry and other curious onlookers from around the world. When he finished, the author wrote Warren Buffett to ask permission to publish. Mr. Buffett wrote back (see reprinted letter on page xx) to say that he had already read the book on the Internet and wished Mr. Miles well. Soon after publication Mr. Buffett ordered copies of the book for the Berkshire Hathaway Board of Directors.

Robert Miles is a shareholder of Berkshire Hathaway and resides in Tampa, Florida.

Index